REFERENCING, UNDERSTANDING PLAGIARISM AND ETHICAL AI

POCKET STUDY SKILLS

Series Editor: **Kate Williams,**
Oxford Brookes University, UK
Illustrations by Sallie Godwin

For the time-pushed student, the *Pocket Study Skills* pack a lot of advice into a little book. Each guide focuses on a single crucial aspect of study giving you step-by-step guidance, handy tips and clear advice on how to approach the important areas which will continually be at the core of your studies.

Published

14 Days to Exam Success (2nd edn)

Analyzing a Case Study

Blogs, Wikis, Podcasts and More

Brilliant Writing Tips for Students (2nd edn)

Completing Your PhD

Doing Research (2nd edn)

Doing Your Literature Review

Getting Critical (3rd edn)

How to Analyze Data

Managing Stress

Planning Your Dissertation (3rd edn)

Planning Your Essay (4th edn)

Planning Your PhD

Posters and Presentations

Reading and Making Notes (3rd edn)

Referencing, Understanding Plagiarism and Ethical AI (3rd edn)

Reflective Writing (2nd edn)

Report Writing (2nd edn)

Science Study Skills

Studying with Dyslexia (3rd edn)

Success in Groupwork (2nd edn)

Successful Applications

Time Management

Using Feedback to Boost Your Grades

Where's Your Evidence?

Writing for University (3rd edn)

Kate Williams and Mary Davis

REFERENCING, UNDERSTANDING PLAGIARISM & ETHICAL AI

THIRD EDITION

BLOOMSBURY ACADEMIC

LONDON · NEW YORK · OXFORD · NEW DELHI · SYDNEY

BLOOMSBURY ACADEMIC
Bloomsbury Publishing Plc, 50 Bedford Square, London, WC1B 3DP, UK
Bloomsbury Publishing Inc, 1359 Broadway, New York, NY 10018, USA
Bloomsbury Publishing Ireland, 29 Earlsfort Terrace, Dublin 2, D02 AY28, Ireland

BLOOMSBURY, BLOOMSBURY ACADEMIC and the Diana logo are trademarks of Bloomsbury Publishing Plc

First published in Great Britain 2009
Second edition published 2017
This edition published 2026

A catalogue record for this book is available from the British Library.

ISBN: PB: 978-1-350-56150-2
          ePDF: 978-1-350-56151-9
          eBook: 978-1-350-56152-6

Series: Pocket Study Skills

Typeset by Integra Software Services Pvt. Ltd.
Printed and bound in India.

For product safety related questions contact productsafety@bloomsbury.com.

To find out more about our authors and books visit www.bloomsbury.com and sign up for our newsletters.

Contents

Acknowledgements

Many people have contributed to this guide – both to the previous editions and to this new edition, refocused to reflect the impact of AI in the research and study experience of both students and tutors. We would like to thank you all.

Thanks to colleagues at Oxford Brookes University: to Richard Persaud (librarian) for his valuable and generous advice, and sharp eye for detail, and Isabel Virgo (librarian) for practical advice on AI tools for research. Special thanks to students who contributed extracts from their work to this edition: Regina, Jay, Alex, Zoe, Besi and Suad.

We owe particular thanks to our reviewers for sharing their experiences in this fast-changing landscape, and whose thoughtful comments, examples and suggestions have helped to shape this new edition.

The authors and publisher wish to thank the following for their kind permission to draw on their materials: Dr John Morley at the University of Manchester for the use of Academic Phrasebank; Julian Eaton, Professor in Global Mental Health, Liverpool School of Tropical Medicine, for the use of the extract that illustrates so many points about writing.

Thanks too to Sallie Godwin for her astute illustrations, and to Helen Caunce and colleagues in the editing and production teams at Bloomsbury for their supportive and creative work with us.

Introduction

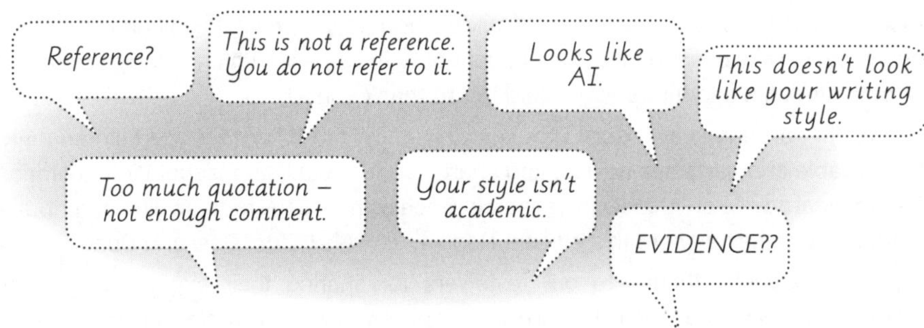

If you have ever had feedback like this on your work and wondered what it means and what you should do about it, then this guide is for you.

Comments like these suggest three things:

- you need to get to grips with referencing
- you need to learn about ethical use of AI
- you are not yet confident about how to draw on other writers and sources in your own writing.

This book is designed to show you:

- how to reference, both in your work and in your reference list
- how to write with confidence: to be able to discuss the work of other writers, and use it to shape the points you want to make in your work
- what plagiarism is and how it can happen. It shows you how to develop good study habits and skills so you don't have to worry about plagiarising by accident
- how to make ethical decisions when you use AI.

This new edition has been extensively revised and updated with new extracts and examples. Guidance on the ethical use of AI runs throughout the book and is the focus of Part 3.

These pointers will show you the difference between:

- using AI as a **tool** to help you (usually ethical) and
- using AI as an **author** or **producer** of work (usually not ethical). The ease of accessing AI has created many more opportunities for extending your research. It also requires you to make choices and presents you with dilemmas about the help you can get with researching and how you use it. **Your work must always be YOUR work!**

About this book

The Harvard referencing style is the main style used in the book. Other referencing styles mentioned in the book are outlined in Chapter 2 and illustrated in the Appendix. Some examples of numeric (Vancouver) referencing style are also included in the text (p. 116).

Part 1: Understanding referencing and ethical use of AI gives an overview of what referencing is and why it matters. It shows how referencing is part of the overall task of understanding, researching, planning and writing an assignment. Using AI ethically is an essential part of this.

Part 2: Writing and referencing shows you how to use sources in your writing, the language to use when you refer to a source – summarising, paraphrasing and using AI in writing and referencing.

Part 3: Understanding plagiarism and ethical use of AI shows you the steps to take in doing 'your own work'. It shows good practice in getting help and using tools, especially AI tools, in ethical ways for paraphrasing, translating and correcting language, so your work remains **your work**.

Part 4: Referencing: the practicalities starts with answers to frequent questions, and gives examples of how to reference the most frequently used sources, both in your text and in your reference list.

Appendix: Other styles of referencing shows how three other referencing styles work, with examples of writing using Numeric (Vancouver pp. 144–6), MHRA (Modern Humanities Research Association pp. 147–50) and APA (American Psychological Association pp. 151–3) styles.

UNDERSTANDING REFERENCING AND ETHICAL USE OF AI

Part 1 gives an overview of what referencing is, why it matters and how it is part of the overall task of understanding, researching, planning and writing an assignment. It highlights how the availability of AI tools is changing the experience of researching for both tutors and students. We point out new opportunities and some of the careful decisions involved in making ethical use of AI.

What's different about writing at university?

Quite a lot is different. That's true no matter where you studied before.

Universities are research environments. Most tutors and lecturers do research of some sort and base their writing on the style used in the books, articles and reports they read for their research: that's where they, too, publish. So it follows that students are also expected to develop the 'academic' style that matches their field of study.

So what is UK 'academic' style?

Well, of course, it varies from subject to subject – dance, science and business are massively different, so the style of writing expected in different areas of study will vary too. But let's try a few generalisations!

You are NOT expected to:

▶ Write out facts, describe events and just summarise your reading or lectures (unless you are expressly asked to – for example, to draw up a timeline, outline, describe a process or observation, or do a 'summary').

You ARE expected to:

▶ Consider everything from several angles: if you are asked to 'outline' different theories, studies or interpretations of 'facts' or events, you will almost certainly be expected to 'discuss' or 'evaluate' them too.

You are ALWAYS expected to:

▶ Show the EVIDENCE for the statements you make. You will need evidence if the statement is a 'fact', or mentions the approach of a particular writer or describes the findings of a study.

The key question this new edition addresses is: where does AI fit in with these expectations?

 REFERENCING, UNDERSTANDING PLAGIARISM AND ETHICAL AI

Using AI

We start with some questions we hear from students about using AI.

Do I cite my use of AI?

Our advice, in line with the Committee on Publication Ethics [COPE] (2023), is that **AI use** must be **acknowledged** but **not cited**.

AI tools are not authors so cannot be cited or added to a reference list, but any use of AI must be acknowledged. Writers – students and researchers – must make clear **how they have used AI in the methods and writing of a paper,** and specify which AI tools they used.

How do I acknowledge my use of AI?

- **Keep a record** of any AI use in the development of your work
- **Acknowledge** your use of AI by clearly communicating this to your reader, on a cover sheet or declaration form, or in an acknowledgements section, at the top of an assignment or on the final page.

For example:

Check with your tutor and assignment instructions, and follow any specific guidance you are given.

Are you using AI as an author or as a tool?

When you use AI as a tool, it enables you to expand your knowledge and skills – you can actively do more and learn more. However, when you use AI as an author or producer of your work, it takes away your knowledge and skills. You become inactive in the process – you do nothing and learn nothing.

Think of using AI as getting on a seesaw – you want to upskill and learn more, not downskill and learn less!

So on to referencing

You provide evidence by telling the reader about the source of your information. The reference is the link between what you write and the evidence on which your writing is based.

Referencing your research turns what you write from being just your thoughts and reactions into something that links your ideas with the writings of other people who have thought and written about the same issue.

It is how you carry out and share your research process.

 REFERENCING, UNDERSTANDING PLAGIARISM AND ETHICAL AI

The essentials of referencing and ethical AI

This chapter gives a quick overview of why and how to reference. From here, you can read on through Part 1 to get a better understanding of referencing as central to your research and writing. AI offers new opportunities for extending your research and for you to show your critical thinking in how you use sources it suggests.

Reference, reference, reference – why do I have to reference everything?

The one overarching reason why you need to reference is to show your reader where the evidence for what you say has come from. This will enable them to:

- go and check the source themselves – **traceability.** Use the DOI (Digital Object Identifier, see box on p. 11) to find the original (especially any sources generated through AI)
- assess the **authenticity** of the source – is the source real or fabricated by AI?
- understand the nature, strengths and limitations of your source – **authority** and **credibility**

- form their own view about the source and the use you make of it – **reliability**. Is there a **bias** in references generated by AI? Do you **trust** the references?

The reader will also be able to see:
- the range of sources you have found and used, from textbooks to the reading list, your independent research – **reach** and **scope**
- your acknowledgment of the value of the efforts and findings of others – **respect**.

All this feeds into your reader's impression of your competence as a researcher and your 'professionalism' as a student. Your tutor will approach your work feeling positive – and that has got to be a good thing!

What does your reader need to know? The bare essentials

The six **strategic questions** make a useful checklist of the information you need to know about your source.

See *Getting Critical* in this series for more on how to use the strategic questions.

Strategic questions

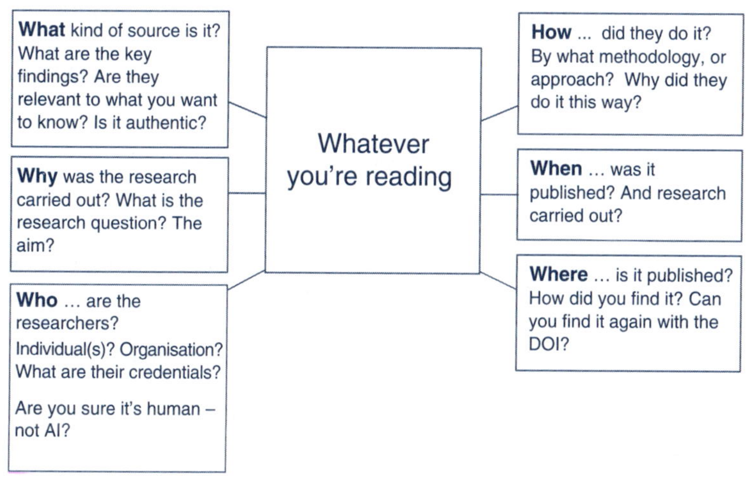

Overarching all these specific questions are the big ones:

So what ... are the implications?

Why does it matter?

The answers you need to give to your reader in your reference are:

Peter Schön, Eva Heinen and **Bendik Manum** wrote an article (published) in 2024. The title is **A scoping review on cycling network connectivity and its effects on cycling.** It was published in the journal *Transport Reviews* in **volume 44, issue 4, pages 912–936**. And this is where you can find it: https://doi.org/10.1080/01441647.2024.2337880

In reference form (author-year Harvard style), this becomes:

1 Author(s) 2 Year 3 Title of article

Schön P, Heinen E and Manum B (2024). A scoping review on cycling network connectivity and its effects on cycling. *Transport Reviews.* 44(4) pp912–936.
https://doi.org/10.1080/01441647.2024.2337880

7 Doi 4 Title of journal 5 Volume + Issue 6 Pages

All referencing styles provide details that answer the same questions – they are just set out differently.

 REFERENCING, UNDERSTANDING PLAGIARISM AND ETHICAL AI

The Digital Object Identifier (DOI or doi) is a unique and permanent number used to locate and identify sources, especially academic and scholarly articles, research reports and datasets, and official or government publications. The DOI will take you directly to the source or 'object' in a search. It's the most reliable way to locate and check the source is genuine.

AI may generate a false (but genuine-looking) DOI. Make sure you check it carefully and that it does take you to the actual article before you include it in your reference list.

Help your reader find your source

It isn't enough just to list everything you have read for an assignment at the end of your writing. At best this just tells your reader that you've been busy; at worst it gives the impression that you've borrowed a list from somewhere else or generated the list by using AI without reading any sources. Your reader will just get annoyed – and you will be the loser.

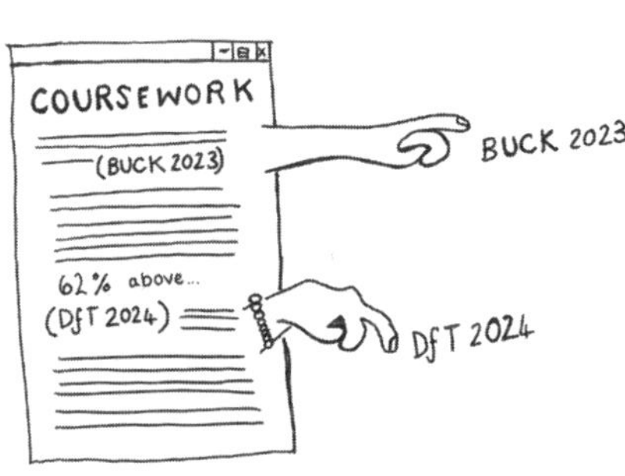

The whole purpose of referencing is to make the process of tracking back to previous research as clear as possible. **Point** your reader to where they can find the support for particular statements at the exact point you draw on the source.

How referencing works

There are many different referencing styles and many more local variations. All operate on the same principles of two linked elements. **In your text** you drop in a signal at the point in your writing where you use a source. This is a 'citation'. It tells the reader two things:

1 that the idea, point or evidence comes from your research

2 where to find that source.

The signal is either:

▶ a **number**[1] or [1] in numeric systems, or

▶ the **author + year** of publication in (most) author-date systems.

 REFERENCING, UNDERSTANDING PLAGIARISM AND ETHICAL AI

In your reference list at the end of your work include ALL the sources you use, giving full details of where to find them. The list can be in either:

▸ **number order** according to where you first use that source in your text (numeric style), or
▸ **alphabetical order** by the author's last name/surname/family name or name of the organisation (author-date style).

Whichever style you use, make sure:
▸ every source you cite in your work is listed in your references, giving the details of where YOU found it (and your reader can find it)
▸ every source listed in your references section is cited in your work.

Styles of referencing

Different disciplines have their preferred way of referencing, often with good reason, sometimes by convention. As a newcomer to the subject, clearly you should follow the models. Some styles have quite precise expectations about how a reference is set out (MHRA for example). Others are more flexible about layout and punctuation. However, even within one subject area – sometimes even in the same department – there can be differences. Individual tutors tend to want students to set out references in the way they themselves do.

Check the style required in your course and module, and make sure you use it consistently – and do consider using reference management/bibliographic software (see Chapter 2).

They are all correct!

Harvard, the style most used in the UK, has no definitive handbook, so there are lots of minor variations in style – and they are all correct!

So what do you do?

Try a bit of self-preservation! Check your course information and module handbook and set your references out in exactly that way. If you use bibliographic software or AI to format or generate references (see p. 17), make sure they all fit the required format – exactly.

What matters and what doesn't?

It doesn't matter if you:
- use or don't use commas, full stops, capitals in titles, underlining/italics. But **be consistent** because different patterns of punctuation annoy readers and could suggest you are over-reliant on cut and paste – or AI-generated lists.

- can't track down some detail, despite your best efforts. It's better to refer to a good source and give the details you have than to leave it out because of a missing detail.

It does matter that you:

- understand the purpose of referencing
- place your in-text link ('citation') at the point you use a source
- give as full a set of details as you can about each source in your reference list
- give up the idea of 'hanging on' to the words used in your source, even if you feel they say it better than you do
- learn to integrate references into your writing style (see Chapter 2)
- pick one style of referencing, and stick to it.

It is unrealistic, however, to expect students to be 100% accurate. World-class professors send books and articles to publishers with incomplete references and copy-editors check and correct missing reference details. Tutors will be looking for authenticity – wanting to see what you have really read and thought about this source material.

This chapter gives a brief overview of the main referencing styles used at university. Most courses will use a style from one of the two 'families' below, or adaptations of these. You don't need to know them all – check the ones used in the courses you take.

This Pocket book uses Harvard except where we explicitly state that we are giving examples in other styles. The **Appendix** (pp142–53) shows specially written extracts with lots of examples to demonstrate how some other widely used referencing styles work:

- **Numeric (Vancouver)** style, widely used in medical and science subject areas (Appendix A pp144–6)
- **MHRA** used in some arts and humanities subjects (Appendix B pp147–50)
- **APA** used in Psychology and related subject areas (Appendix C pp151–3)

We stress the importance of ensuring your references are accurate and consistent. A key strategy for achieving this is to use referencing software.

Reference management / bibliographic software: why use it?

It helps you **keep track** of what you have read. It

- **saves you time:** it avoids having to type out each reference manually
- ensures your referencing is **consistent and accurate:** less room for error
- **helps to keep your research organised:** you can store your references in one place in a systematic way.

The most used software packages are:

- Endnote
- Mendeley
- Zotero
- Refworks, available via university libraries.

Check out your library for recommendations and advice on using this software.

Adapted from UCL guidance, CC BY NC-SA 4.0, with additional permission from UCL.

Referencing styles

Family 1: In-text author name referencing styles

In your work cite the **surname** of the author(s) at the point you draw on a source and the **year of publication** (in brackets).

In your references list give the full details of each source listed in alphabetical order (by first author) so your reader can find it by surname.

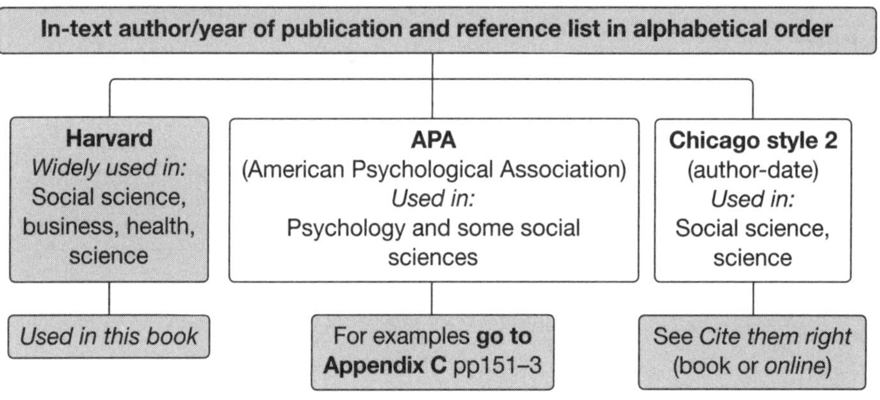

A Harvard reference	
In your work	**In your reference list**
… the importance of well-connected cycling infrastructure in encouraging people … (Schön, Heinen and Manum, 2024)	Schön P, Heinen E and Manum B (2024). A scoping review on cycling network connectivity and its effects on cycling. *Transport Reviews.* 44(4) pp912–936. https://doi.org/10.1080/01441647.2024.2337880

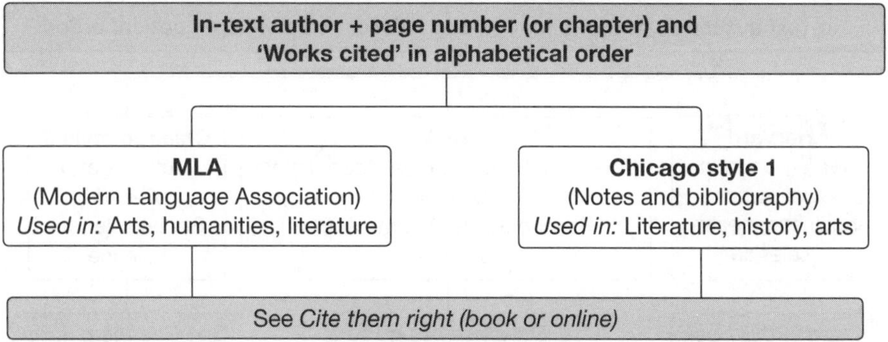

In-text author + page number (or chapter) and 'Works cited' in alphabetical order

MLA (Modern Language Association) *Used in:* Arts, humanities, literature	**Chicago style 1** (Notes and bibliography) *Used in:* Literature, history, arts

See *Cite them right (book or online)*

Family 2: In-text numeric styles and reference list in number order

In your work you use a number, in superscript[7] or brackets, round (7) or square [7] at the point you draw on a source.

In your references give the full details of each source in number order, with the first source you use listed as 1, the second as 2 and so on. Each source keeps this number for all later citations.

 **REFERENCING, UNDERSTANDING PLAGIARISM AND ETHICAL AI**

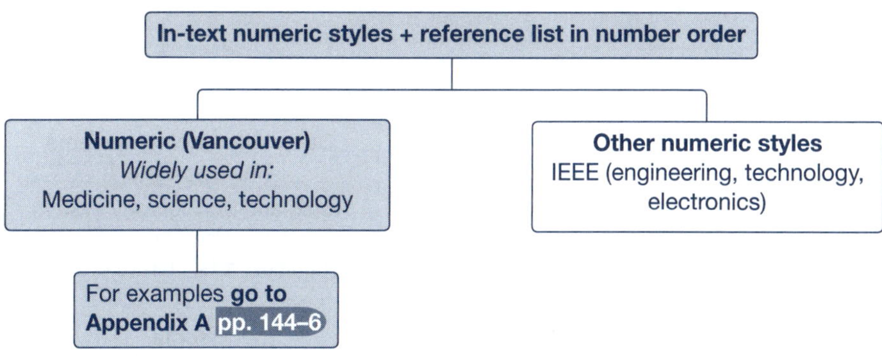

| A numeric (Vancouver) reference ||
In your work	In your reference list
… the importance of well-connected cycling infrastructure[7] in encouraging people …	7 Schön P, Heinen E and Manum B (2024). A scoping review on cycling network connectivity and its effects on cycling. *Transport Reviews*. 44(4) pp912–936. https://doi.org/10.1080/01441647.2024.2337880

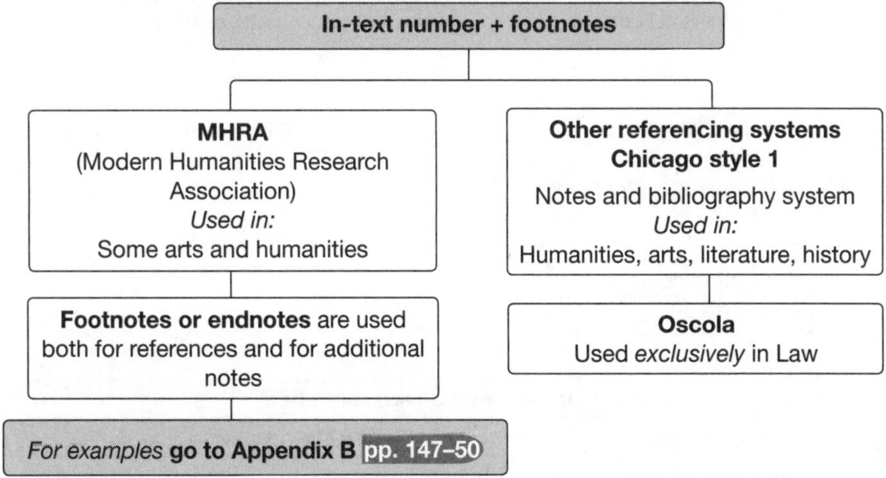

In-text number + footnotes

MHRA	**Other referencing systems**

MHRA
(Modern Humanities Research Association)
Used in:
Some arts and humanities

Other referencing systems
Chicago style 1
Notes and bibliography system
Used in:
Humanities, arts, literature, history

Footnotes or endnotes are used both for references and for additional notes

Oscola
Used *exclusively* in Law

For examples **go to Appendix B** pp. 147–50

You may also be required to list your sources in a bibliography at the end of your work.

Read your course materials carefully to make sure you are clear about the style of referencing your tutor expects for that particular module or course. You may well be given guidance and helpful models to use. If so, do use them!

Your references will show your research footprints and be the record of your research. Record them carefully as you go, and connect each source with notes you make.

 REFERENCING, UNDERSTANDING PLAGIARISM AND ETHICAL AI

Referencing is a great invention. It enables researchers of all levels, from eminent professor to first-year student, to show and share their research with their readers. Your reader will be able to see how your research has informed your thinking and understanding.

Throughout your research, keep careful records, notes, and the full reference of every source you check out. Using reference management software will make this much easier (see p. 17).

You'll do a lot of work before you get anywhere near planning and writing your assignment or essay. Your references are the record of your research. Look after them!

Choosing your sources

Before you start looking for sources to research your assignment or essay, you need to be clear about what exactly the task or question is asking you.

For tips on making effective notes, see *Reading and Making Notes* and for the stages in essay writing see *Planning Your Essay* in this series.

Books, journal articles and **websites** are the essential sources of information, ideas and interpretation. But you may need to consult other types of sources current in your subject area and relevant to your task.

For any source you have to decide if it is good for your purpose.

Try using the **strategic questions** (see p. 9 as a checklist) to help you evaluate the source and decide if you want to explore it further.

What?	How?
Why?	When?
Who?	Where?

Then ask the big question: **SO WHAT?**

▸ So … what are the implications? What do these answers tell me about the nature and quality of the source? Can I rely on it?

▸ So … is this source relevant to me and my purpose? How might it be useful to me?

 REFERENCING, UNDERSTANDING PLAGIARISM AND ETHICAL AI

Make notes … your own notes in your own words:

- be clear about what is the source and what's yours
- record the source alongside the key points you record
- think as you go.

This is when you process information, see different perspectives and begin to think about what you have read – and how it addresses the question or task you have been set. You are upskilling and learning.

Don't

- have lots of tabs open
- cut and paste directly into your assignment.

Here you are downskilling (see p. 4), reducing your learning.

You need to be able to show what comes directly from the source and what value you have added in your comments, informed by your reading and learning.

See *Getting Critical* in this series.

The research process

Collecting your sources, making notes and recording your references systematically starts way back, well before you start writing. Consider using referencing software from the start.

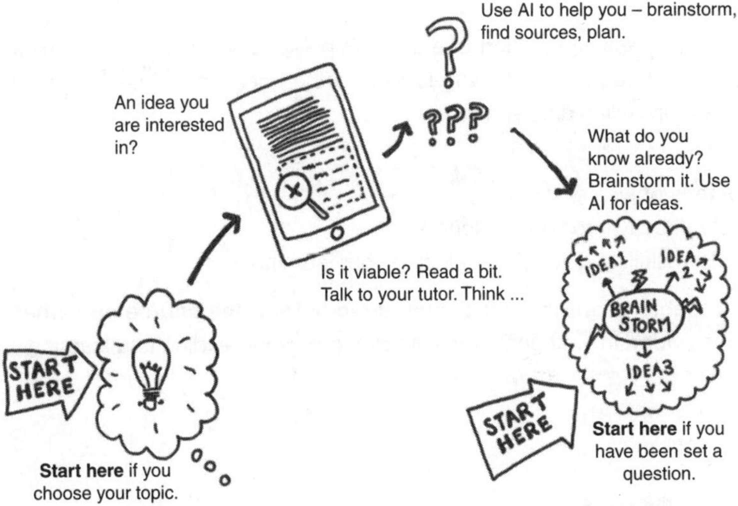

 REFERENCING, UNDERSTANDING PLAGIARISM AND ETHICAL AI

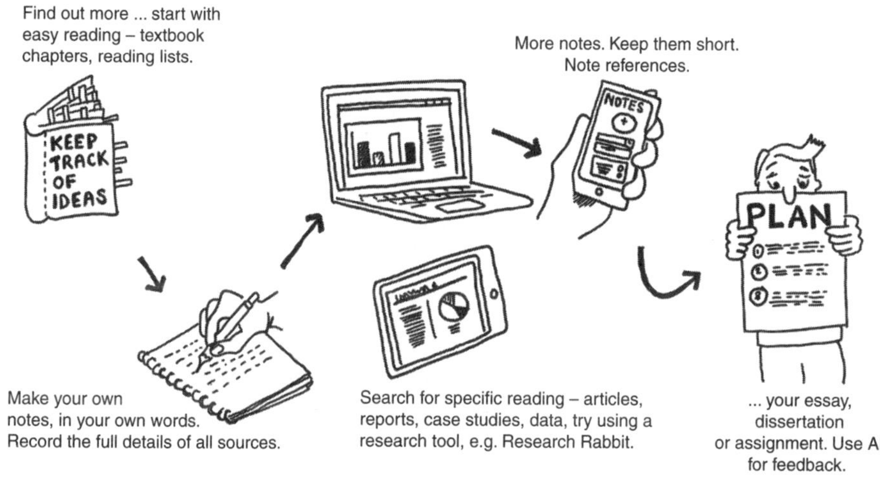

Find out more ... start with easy reading – textbook chapters, reading lists.
KEEP TRACK OF IDEAS
More notes. Keep them short. Note references.
NOTES
PLAN
Make your own notes, in your own words. Record the full details of all sources.
Search for specific reading – articles, reports, case studies, data, try using a research tool, e.g. Research Rabbit.
... your essay, dissertation or assignment. Use AI for feedback.

Research tools example: Research Rabbit

Research Rabbit is a free tool which enables you to collect and connect references through keyword searches or by entering article titles. It connects sources that cite each other in clusters on a visual map. It can be a useful way to start a literature review search or to look at connections after finding some initial sources.

The map is live and interactive and you can select individual references to examine the connections with others.

You can be confident that this tool is ethical – it gives you a visual connection between references, but it does not generate text for you.

It is your responsibility to read the sources and make decisions about how to use them.

Notice the connections between authors/articles shown by the lines connecting the bubbles. The more linking lines, the more connections.

We started with the source: Cook S, Stevenson L, Aldred R, Kendall M, Cohen T (2022). More than walking and cycling: what is 'active travel'? We can see the connections with other authors and articles.

 REFERENCING, UNDERSTANDING PLAGIARISM AND ETHICAL AI

Similar Work

Diverging Mobilities?: Devolution, Transport and Policy Innovation

**Buck 2023
Disruption, and opportunity to facilitate long-term modal shift to cycling?**
Active travel studies

**Cook 2022
More than walking and cycling: what is 'active travel'?**
Transport Policy

**Buehler and Pucher 2023
COVID-19 and cycling: a review of the literature on changes in cycling levels and government policy 2019 to 2022**
Transport Reviews

**Goel 2022
Cycling behaviour in 17 countries across 6 continents**
Transport Reviews

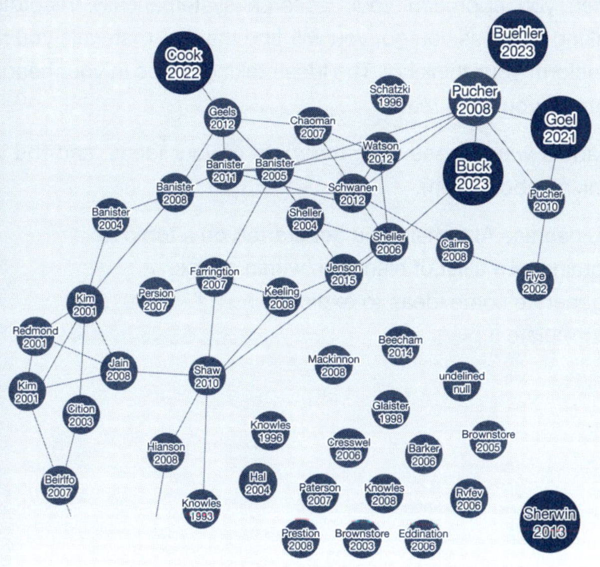

Transforming sources into ideas

When you approach your research systematically, recording your references and making notes as you go, you will find that the materials you read gradually shape and transform your thinking. The ideas taking shape in your head have roots back into the material you have read.

Readers want to see both the roots of your ideas, and the value you have added in thinking about them.

You can use AI to help you get started on a topic to:
- brainstorm a list of elements within a topic
- generate some ideas to explore
- formulate a plan.

Then you need to do some thinking and evaluating to develop the topic further – ensuring you remain the author and use AI as an assistive tool.

In Chapter 4 you can see this research process in action in an extract that shows a student's research and thinking.

This chapter shows an extract from the literature review of an undergraduate dissertation. The writer, Alex, uses references in a way that shows exactly where he got his information from. He leaves clear footprints:

- **in his work**, at the exact point where he uses each source, pointing you to
- the **full reference list** at the end showing you, the reader, where to find each source yourself.

In this extract from his dissertation, Alex used several articles suggested by Research Rabbit (see p. 28) along with other sources he found useful.

2.1 Mobility cultures

The advent of mass motorisation across western civilisation had a major impact on cycling as an everyday method of transportation. In the UK, cycling levels peaked in 1949 when 24 billion kilometres were travelled by bike, 37% of all traffic (Docherty and Shaw 2008), and similarly high levels were experienced in the Netherlands and Denmark (Goel et al. 2021). By the 1970s, cycling had reduced dramatically across Europe: by about two-thirds in a sample of Dutch, Danish and German cities and to 1% of modal share of travelling miles in the UK (van Wee, Annema and Banister 2023) as the car culture dominated transport policies.

In the second half of the twentieth century, however, the pattern of cycling in mainland Europe and the UK diverged markedly. Political pressure in the Netherlands led to a dramatic reversal of transportation policy and the re-establishment of the bicycle culture as part of the Dutch national identity (Carstensen and Ebert 2012).

No such change in attitudes to cycling took place in the UK. In the early 2000s, despite initiatives to broaden the appeal of cycling such as 'Active travel' (Cook et al. 2022), levels of cycling remained low…

This changed radically in the period of Covid-19, when restrictions and lockdowns led to a dramatic increase in cycling. As in other countries, people in the UK cycled for leisure and fitness, not for commuting to work (Buehler and Pucher 2023). This peaked in March 2021, with an increase of 62% above 2013 levels (DfT 2024). Yet, as traffic 'rebounded to normal levels' (Buck 2023), cycling levels dropped to near pre-pandemic levels. A major shift in traffic management and cycling infrastructure, in particular the connectivity of infrastructure (Schön, Heinen and Manum 2024), is needed if cycling levels are to rise in the UK.

Many thanks to Alex Neisig Moller (Planning student) for his kind permission to adapt this extract from his dissertation.

Here are the references to sources Alex used in this extract, Harvard style, in alphabetical order by author:

 REFERENCING, UNDERSTANDING PLAGIARISM AND ETHICAL AI

References

Buck M (2023). Disruption, an opportunity to facilitate long-term modal shift to cycling? Stories, lessons and reflections from the COVID-19 pandemic. *Active Travel Studies*. 3(2) pp1–20. https://doi.org/10.16997/ats.1221

Buehler R and Pucher J (2023). COVID-19 and cycling: a review of the literature on changes in cycling levels and government policies from 2019 to 2022. *Transport Reviews*. 44(2) pp299–344. https://doi.org/10.1080/01441647.2023.2205178

Carstensen TA and Ebert A (2012). Cycling cultures in northern Europe. In Parkin J (ed). *Cycling and sustainability*. Bingley: Emerald, pp23–58.

Cook S, Stevenson L, Aldred R, Kendall M, Cohen T (2022). More than walking and cycling: What is 'active travel'? *Transport Policy*.126, pp151–161. https://doi.org/10.1016/j.tranpol.2022.07.015

Department for Transport (DfT) (2024). Official statistics: Cycling traffic index, England. (Available at https://www.gov.uk/government/statistics/cycling-index-england/cycling-index-england.) (Accessed 1 March 2025).

Docherty I and Shaw J (2008). *Traffic Jam: ten years of 'sustainable' transport in the UK*. Bristol: Policy.

Goel R, Goodman A, Aldred R, Nakamura R, Tatah L, Garcia LMT, Zapata-Diomedi B (2022). Cycling behaviour in 17 countries across 6 continents: levels of cycling, who cycles, for what purpose, and how far? *Transport Reviews*. 42(1) pp58–81. https://doi.org/10.1080/01441647.2021.1915898

Schön P, Heinen E, Manum B (2024). A scoping review on cycling network connectivity and its effects on cycling. *Transport Reviews*. 44(4) pp912–936. https://doi.org/10.1080/01441647.2024.2337880

van Wee B, Annema JA, Banister D, Pudãne B, eds. (2023). *The transport system and transport policy: an introduction*. Cheltenham: Edward Elgar.

The test! Tracking Alex's research footprints

Remember why the reader needs a reference (pp. 7–8)?

1 Can I, the reader, find the source?

2 What kind of source is it?

3 How does the writer (Alex) use it?

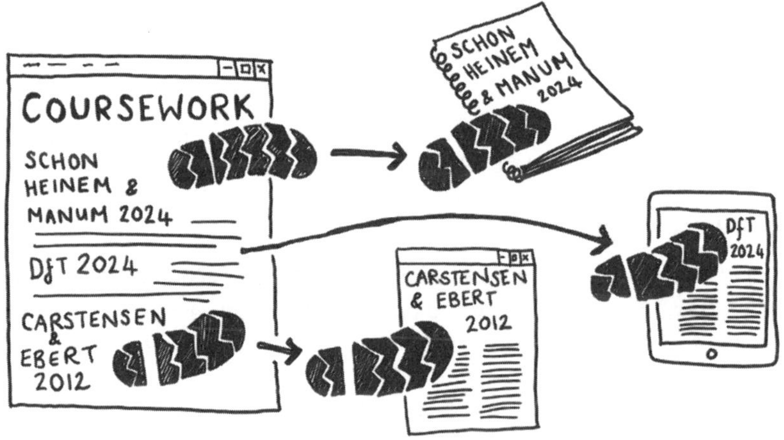

How easy is it to follow the trail? Are these credible sources?

Here is the follow-up to some of Alex's references.

Source 1: Buehler and Pucher (2023)

Finding it: You can find it quickly with its doi.

What kind of source? A highly reliable, academic, peer-reviewed journal article. Every article in a 'peer-reviewed' article has been read by specialists in the specific research area before publication. The researchers themselves reviewed 100 peer-reviewed articles in their study.

Well used? Yes, very. Alex can be sure that this is reliable, authoritative research into the unprecedented period of COVID-19.

Source 2: Carstensen and Ebert 2012

Finding it: This chapter is in a book edited by Parkin. A search in the library catalogue ('Parkin cycling') listed both the printed book and the eBook (available to view online or download). As they are identical, the writer did not need to specify which version he used.

What kind of source? It's a big (expensive!) textbook, with three major parts, each with several chapters by different authors.

Well used? Yes – it is quite old but a valid source for Alex's historical context of cycling trends in Europe.

Source 3: Department for Transport (2024)

Finding it: The title was enough to find it immediately via a Google search.

What kind of source? Authoritative government statistics based on the latest census in the UK, published by the government's Office of National Statistics.

Well used? Yes, very. A primary source for up-to-date statistics.

A reference shows your research footprints

- **Printed materials** exist in time and space. The reference gives the information to be able to find it on the library shelf, if you are lucky enough to have a library that stocks it – but you don't need to set foot in a library to access most of these materials.
- **Books,** especially popular textbooks, have their eBook version to read online or download. You can log in from anywhere.

- **Academic databases** are trustworthy sources – the location is fixed and they don't move around like other online sources. When an article has a doi you can find any article in a database by clicking on it.
- The **internet** is vast, mobile and open to everyone. Two points to think about:
  - *Could I or my reader find it again?* Things move around – so include enough details to find it, wherever it has moved to.
  - *Is it any good?* Ask questions about anything you find … use the six strategic questions (p9) as a checklist.

Enjoy becoming a researcher!

 REFERENCING, UNDERSTANDING PLAGIARISM AND ETHICAL AI

WRITING AND REFERENCING

Referencing is part of writing for a researcher or student: it's not something you add later. It is through your reading and research that you gain knowledge and understanding, and it is in your writing that you show your thinking. Referencing shows your research footprints, remember? (see pp. 39–40).

You can use AI as an assistive tool in research and referencing – to help you:

- find sources and see connections between them (see Research Rabbit example p. 28)
- understand key ideas from sources through summaries
- format your references in the style required by your course/institution (by using reference management software).

Part 2 outlines some of the ways to include your research and reading in your writing – with careful referencing.

Why use the research of other authors?

You may want to:

- use an author as an **authority** to support what you are saying
- introduce someone else's **perspective** that you want to discuss
- provide **evidence** of a trend or development you are discussing
- show differences between **experts' views** and interpretations
- show the difference between an **author's views** and **your own.**

Making notes

Before you read an article in depth … get an overview.

Look at the **outline**, (usually positioned on the left of your screen in an online journal article). It gives you the route map of the article. Here is the outline of an article by Eaton et al. (pp60–1) – a helpful start point for **notemaking**.

Abstract	The **framework** – key summary
Keywords	Helpful search words for further research
Introduction	**Essential reading** – shows you the direction and issues of the article
Body (sub-headings) - The impact of international health worker migration on health - Impact on economic development - International workforce recruitment commitments - Do migrants return to their home countries with skills and experience to offer? - Remittances	**Gives an overview** of the five key areas of the content of the article – useful headings for notes and summary
Conclusion	**Take-away points**

And when do you need to reference?

You need to reference when you:

▸ use facts, figures or specific details you pick from somewhere to support a point you're making – you **report**

▸ use a framework or model another author has devised – you **acknowledge**

▸ use the exact words of your source – you **quote**

▸ restate in your own words a specific point, finding or argument an author has made – you **paraphrase**

▸ sum up in a phrase or a few sentences a whole article or chapter, a key finding/ conclusion or a section – you **summarise**.

 REFERENCING, UNDERSTANDING PLAGIARISM AND ETHICAL AI

Common knowledge

You don't need to reference if you:

- believe that what you are writing is widely known and accepted as 'fact' or **'common knowledge'** in your subject
- can honestly say, 'I didn't have to research anything to know that!'.

But

If finding it out did take effort, show the reader the research you did by referencing it.

> **Try this!**
>
> If you write something down which you can imagine someone else asking questions about, like 'Really?' 'Who says?' 'Why's that?' 'That's a lot!' 'How do you know that?' ... then you must have found it out from somewhere, and you should show your reader where it comes from – in a reference.

Report

When you report on specific information you have found and which you now need to use – like a fact, event, figure, map or date – you bring it into your text and give the

- in-text reference (or 'citation')
- full reference in the references section.

In your work	Reference list
In the early 2000s, despite initiatives to broaden the appeal of cycling such as 'active travel' (Cook at al. 2022), levels of cycling remained low …	Cook S, Stevenson L, Aldred R, Kendall M, Cohen T. (2022). More than walking and cycling: what is 'active travel'? *Transport Policy.* 126, Sept, pp151– 161. Available at: https://doi.org/10.1016/j.tranpol.2022.07.015

It is helpful but not essential to include the page number for specific points or numbers.

Acknowledge

When you locate a source, it takes a little time to work out how you will use it. First you have to understand it, then you engage with it as you think about it.

The Open University (2008, p9) described the progression when you analyse, evaluate and synthesise as 'higher order thinking skills'.

In *Getting Critical* in this series, this idea gains an image.

The stairway image is my idea (KW) but I owe the Open University for the inspiration. It helped me to organise my ideas for that Pocket book, so it is important to acknowledge the source. It is also **good practice** to **acknowledge** a debt to whoever came up with the model, template or framework you use – especially if you develop or change it.

Quote

'To copy out or repeat (a passage, statement etc.) from a book, document, speech etc. with some indication that one is giving the words of another'.

(Oxford University Press 2007)

Only use a quote when it is especially important for your reader to see and appreciate the precise wording of the original. You may decide to do this:

1 to provide the reader with the original when you are discussing the text in detail (like in poetry, literary or historical criticism, regulations, reports or policy documents)
2 because the writer (or speaker) is eminent/surprising/authoritative
3 because the words themselves are vivid/surprising/a catchphrase and you'd lose the impact if you tried to explain or paraphrase it. Use quotations sparingly.

George Orwell's advice to writers is as relevant today as it was in the England of the 1940s: 'Never use a long word where a short word will do.' (Orwell 1946 p169). In the 21st century, students …	You can use a quote for any of the situations above. This quote illustrates all three: - we (the readers) have the words in front of us (1) - the writer is eminent (2) - the words are sharp and unique (3).

Quoted extracts – other people's words – can illustrate a point you make. They are not an alternative to explaining a point in your own words. Using quotes in this way can

- give the impression that you don't understand the point well enough to explain it
- lock you into describing, and stop you from showing critical thinking in your comments.

Short quotations (less than two lines)

To use short quotes well:

- run the quotation into your text so that it reads smoothly
- use quotation marks, single or double, as long as you are consistent
- give the page number of the original in your in-text reference, so your reader can find it easily
- give the full reference in your references section.

 REFERENCING, UNDERSTANDING PLAGIARISM AND ETHICAL AI

In your work	Reference list
Ofsted (2023/4 p21) states that attendance issues have 'deepened' since the pandemic and that, for many children, education has become 'fragmented'. Despite this, the positive …	Ofsted (2023/24). *The Annual Report of His Majesty's Chief Inspector of Education, Children's Services and Skills 2023/24.* Available at: https://www.gov.uk/government/publications/ofsted-annual-report-202324-education-childrens-services-and-skills (Accessed 1 July 2025)

Quotation marks are used so your reader can distinguish at a glance between your words and the words of the other writer (or speaker). Your quote must use the exact wording, punctuation and spelling of the original.

Long quotations (two lines or more)

Typically a long quotation is used for an extract from a key text you want to discuss (for example, a policy document). To use long quotes well:

▸ indent the passage – so no need for quotation marks (don't use them)
▸ give the in-text link (citation) to the reference list at the end of the quotation (author-date or numeric), and the page number(s) of the original

See also *Getting Critical* In this series for 'quote hopping'.

- use […] to show some words have been left out of the quotation
- give the full reference in the references section.

Avoid going above five or six lines of original text – readers find long extracts too distracting when they are trying to follow your ideas.

> The government's policy on childhood obesity (April 2022) directly addresses health professionals:
>
> > Healthcare professionals play an important role in supporting families to take action. They can also influence the general population by delivering whole systems approaches to tackle excess weight, and reduce drivers of excess calorie intake and sedentary lifestyles. (Office for Health Improvement and Disparities 2022).
>
> The document points out that children living with obesity are more likely to become adults living with obesity …
>
> **Reference**
>
> Office for Health Improvement and Disparities (2022). *Childhood obesity: applying All Our Health*. Available at: https://www.gov.uk/government/publications/childhood-obesity-applying-all-our-health/childhood-obesity-applying-all-our-health (Accessed 1 July 2025).

Quote + comment

The key thing about deciding to use a quote is:

> If it's worth a quote, it's worth a comment!

Don't just drop a quote and run off to your next point. Tell your reader why you think those words are special: what the quote might mean, how it is interpreted, what is interesting/surprising/new/influential about the quoted comment. This doesn't have to be a big deal – see the boxed examples above.

Too much quoting

Generally students quote too much, and comment too little. Do you?

Try this!

- Ask yourself: *Are these* words *somehow special?* If they aren't, then report them, paraphrase them, summarise them – plus comment on them!
- Ask yourself: *Is this* extract *somehow special?* If it isn't, then report it, paraphrase it, summarise it – plus comment on it!
- Read a section of a couple of journal articles on your reading list. Count the quotes. Not many? This is telling you something.

As a general rule, if you find yourself quoting more than a couple of words more than once or twice per paragraph, or if you find yourself taking a couple of lines from any one source more than once or twice, then you are probably overdoing the quotes. Try and find another way to include the point or discussion. This (of course) does not apply if it's a piece of writing where quoting is half the point, such as an essay about poetry, or discussing a policy document.

Paraphrasing

'To express the meaning of (a word, phrase etc) in other words'.

(Oxford University Press 2007)

Paraphrasing is about expressing the **meaning** of short extracts – the definition suggests a single word or a short phrase, but it can be longer than this. To express meaning in your own words you first have to understand it, and then find the words to express it.

Paraphrasing is hard work. Keep it for short extracts, when the idea is useful to your argument or what you want to say, but the words are not special. Where the words are special, quote (briefly) + comment.

  REFERENCING, UNDERSTANDING PLAGIARISM AND ETHICAL AI

How to paraphrase

Reading

- Read a larger section – don't try to paraphrase line by line as you go along.
- Focus on the ideas, not the words.

Making notes

- Imagine explaining it to a friend – a useful way to find your own words.
- Tell your reader what you want them to see in it – don't just drop it in the text and run off to your next point!

Writing

- Aim to end up with a shorter version than the original.

Check it

- Put the in-text reference as close as you can to your paraphrase, and give the page number(s) of the original.
- List the full details in your references.

Example

Jay has read an original source (Eriksen) from his reading list and wants to discuss it in his essay.

<table>
<tr><td>Jay wrote ...</td><td>The reader sees ...</td></tr>
<tr><td>Eriksen (2002) comments that the term 'race' is of 'dubious descriptive value' (p4), first, because so many people in the world are of mixed race, and second, because the variation within a single 'racial' group (Eriksen's punctuation) is greater than the variation between different groups.</td><td>A close paraphrase of a short section of a paragraph. Key words are quoted: they are 'special' – they sum up the author's view.

Jay explains the two reasons from a longer paragraph in his own words. The reasons are important to understand, but the words of the original are not. By picking the points he shows his understanding – and shortens it.</td></tr>
<tr><td>Reference
Eriksen TH (2002). Ethnicity and nationalism (2nd edn). London: Pluto.</td><td></td></tr>
</table>

Problems with paraphrasing

Problems often arise when students try to capture summaries by other authors and re-express them in their own words. A textbook or article may summarise the findings or arguments of other studies so that the reader gets an overview of debates or research in that field. The problem for you, the reader, is that you haven't read these other studies, so you don't actually know what they do say – apart from what the text in front of you says they say.

 REFERENCING, UNDERSTANDING PLAGIARISM AND ETHICAL AI

Here paraphrasing is tricky. Without really knowing what the original source said, it is difficult to express it in a different way to how the textbook author put it. This can lead to superficial changes that are, or come close to being, plagiarism (see p. 78).

So try and avoid paraphrasing sources you have not read yourself. Summarise, report on specific findings and quote + comment on special words. And always show where the ideas came from – with a reference.

Paraphrasing and AI

GenAI tools can generate an instant alternative version of any text. They seem ideal for paraphrasing. **BUT think carefully:**

Where do YOU draw the line between using AI as
- producer or author of a text? and
- an assistive tool? (see AI seesaw p. 5)

Think about:
- the **amount you are relying** on AI: using AI to produce a complete new version of an assignment (total paraphrase) is not ethical, as you are no longer the author of the text;
- **how you are using it**. Using AI to paraphrase a sentence or section from a text, is using it as a tool. You, as author, are still in control of the text.

For more on paraphrasing and AI see Part 3

Summarise

'To state briefly or succinctly'. (Oxford University Press 2007)

Summary is key. It is the most efficient way of capturing your research in your writing. Use it if you want to capture, for example:

- key outcomes of a study
- an argument
- the approach taken to (…).

First, do your reading. Read a page or two. Look up and think: 'What, in a nutshell, does this tell me that I can use in what I am saying?'

Then write it down, in your own words. Keep it short.

Summarising and AI

GenAI tools are often used to summarise texts. Getting an instant summary of a long text can

- save a lot of time and
- enable you to get an overview of different sources quickly.

It can be a helpful overview BUT if this is all you do, you will not be doing your reading and gaining knowledge.

 REFERENCING, UNDERSTANDING PLAGIARISM AND ETHICAL AI

> **Ethical use of AI** is generating summaries of texts to help you to choose which ones to read. AI is an assistive tool in your research. You are upskilling as a researcher.

> **Unethical use of AI** is taking the AI-generated summaries and putting them directly in your assignment, instead of reading, interpreting and crafting your own understanding. Here, AI is replacing you as the author and producer of the assignment. You are downskilling as a researcher (see p. 4).

Key steps in making a summary

- Pick out the **key points** from the original. Look at the **outline** of the article for an overview (see p. 43).
- Make your **own notes**, in your own words. When you also include phrases from the original, put them in **quotes in your notes** so you can distinguish between the original (which you will need to reference) and your own comments. Add what you think is important about the point or quote to remind yourself when you come back to it.
- **Record full details** of each source.

Then, when you write:

- use your own words (The original will be far too long!)
- put the in-text reference as close as you can to the summary (before or after)
- list the full details in the references
- if you are capturing meaning that arises from several pages of reading, you don't need to give page numbers. If you are summarising a specific point from a single page, then give the page number (if there is one) of where exactly you got it from.

Summarising key findings: professionals at work

Below is an extract from a journal article that shows how experienced researchers summarise – in very few words – key findings from other articles to provide evidence for the argument they are making.

Each paragraph in Eaton et al.'s article (pp. 60–1) develops one point. String these together, and a series of well-supported and evidenced points quickly becomes an argument.

Summarising shorter sections

You don't have to summarise whole articles in just a few words, of course! You can summarise any material you want to use, with any level of detail you choose. But the process is the same. Ask yourself: what is it they are saying, in short? Is it useful to me? Then bring the point into your work, re-express it in your own words, show where it came from and comment on it.

The authors wrote ...	**The reader sees ...**
The valuable contribution made by health staff who migrate to work in other countries is incontrovertible. It compensates for local shortfalls in personnel, and improves the quality of care that can be provided. Many high-income country health systems (including the UK) have become increasingly reliant on personnel trained abroad. They could not currently function effectively without them. There are, however, substantial consequences for the source countries where these personnel trained. In this article, we document the scale of migration from countries where health systems are often poorly staffed and argue that alternatives to such large scale recruitment of overseas health staff must be found	*First paragraph, topic sentence – the writers set the context: the 'valuable contribution' made by health staff migrating from poorer to richer countries.*
	powerful summary of dependence of UK
	Topic sentence states the main argument.
	Authors point to the contribution of their research.
	... leading to argument for alternatives ...
Academic literature spanning decades has documented the damage that the medical brain-drain does to health	*Research 'spanning decades' – supports the argument that this is a long-standing problem. (note references to 2008 studies).*

services in poorer countries (Beine, Doquier and Rapoport 2008); Mills et al. (2008). WHO reports have repeatedly drawn attention to the critical shortages of health workers across Africa, the Middle East and Asia (WHO 2020). Most low- and middle-income countries (LMICs) have much poorer health indices than OECD countries (OECD 2021), and the WHO has estimated that countries with less than 23 health workers (doctors, nurses, midwives) per 10,000 population are unable to deliver essential health services (WHO 2016). … The loss of medical staff and resulting high levels of maternal and child mortality also has a high economic cost to the poorest countries … (Saluja et al. 2020)

Source: Eaton J, Baingana F, Abdulaziz M, Obindo T, Skuse D, Jenkins R (2023). The negative impact of global health worker migration, and how it can be addressed. *Public Health.* 225, Dec 2023, pp254–257. https://doi.org/10.1016/j.puhe.2023.09.014

For an example of numeric (Vancouver) style of referencing, (used in science, medical and related subjects) see the extract from this article (Appendix A pp. 145–6)

 REFERENCING, UNDERSTANDING PLAGIARISM AND ETHICAL AI

From this introduction, the reader (you!) can see the argument and evidence before you. If you want to follow up on the topic, you can start by checking out the sources the authors used. That's what referencing and becoming a researcher is about!

Referencing, writing and argument

Regina at work

Regina is writing an essay on training and recruitment of health professionals – doctors and nurses – in the UK. She found the article by Eaton et al. and was rather shocked by it. She read it closely and looked at some of the sources they cited.

In her discussion of the problem (of shortage of staff in the NHS) Regina wants to give her reader a more detailed account of Eaton et al.'s argument and the wider debate about staffing the NHS.

Regina wrote …	**The reader sees …**
Securing enough health workers to staff UK hospitals has led to widespread recruitment from other, poorer countries for decades. Eaton et al. (2023) argue that this 'skills drain' (p256) acts as a huge subsidy for richer countries when the costs of training are considered. Their analysis of WHO data demonstrates the impact of the loss of health workers on child and maternal deaths. The loss of medical and nursing staff is so severe that many of the poorest countries are unable to provide basic health services to their populations.	*Topic sentence: Regina outlines the problem of understaffing and recruitment for the NHS in the UK.* *She picks out Eaton et. al's key message –'skills-drain' (strong phrase, quoted).* *– and refers to their use of primary data to show impact.* *Strong restatement of argument to conclude paragraph.*
Eaton et al. dismiss the argument that doctors and nurses coming to the UK develop skills and experience they take back to their countries of origin, describing the numbers of doctors and nurses who return permanently as 'vanishingly small' (p256). They also	*Regina shows how Eaton et al. present their argument and quotes a powerful key phrase.*

point out that while remittances sent home are considerable, the cost of the loss of trained doctors and nurses creates a far greater subsidy from poor to richer countries.

Eaton et al. conclude that to reduce the huge health inequalities between richer and poorer countries, wealthier countries like the UK must increase the number of doctors and nurses they train, and promised international investment in poorer countries must be implemented.

From Regina's reference list:
Eaton J, Baingana F, Abdulaziz M, Obindo T, Skuse D, Jenkins R (2023). The negative impact of global health worker migration, and how it can be addressed. *Public Health*. 225, Dec 2023, pp254–257. https://doi.org/10.1016/j.puhe.2023.09.014

Summary is THE most useful skill in writing about your research. Combined with short quotes and examples, it gives a powerful flavour of the research you are reading, and offers a ready way for you to draw material into your argument.

6 Write with confidence

Regina (p62) and Alex (p32) are both capable student writers. As readers we are interested in what they have to say. This chapter takes a close look at strategies, structures and language a writer can use – and inspire confidence in their readers.

Putting references in your text

As soon as your reader starts thinking these things, then as a writer you have a problem. You need to get in quicker and show your reader whose ideas you are writing about.

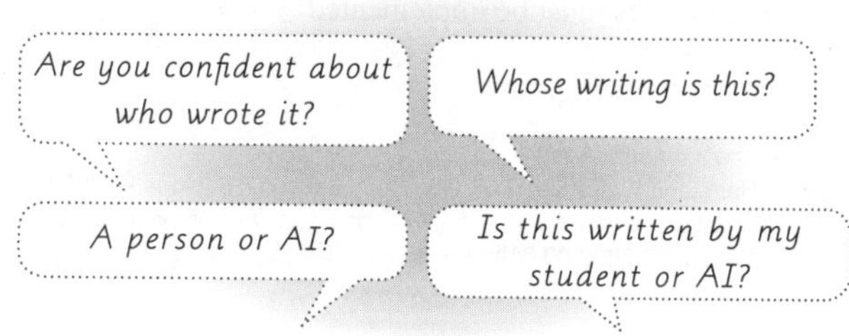

 REFERENCING, UNDERSTANDING PLAGIARISM AND ETHICAL AI

Two styles for writing (Harvard style)

Style 1: Focus on the *ideas*

In this writing style, you want to focus on the ideas and research findings that provide evidence for your argument. The author(s) name does not naturally appear in your writing so you add the author(s) and year in brackets to show the reader where ideas or evidence come from. The brackets hardly interrupt the flow, and academic readers are well used to this.

Below is the extract from Eaton et al. again, this time with the key points shown in bold, and the in-text references just there in brackets.

Academic literature spanning decades has documented the damage that the **medical brain-drain** does to health services in **poorer countries** (Beine, Doquier and Rapoport 2008; Mills et al. 2008). WHO reports have repeatedly drawn attention to the **critical shortages of health workers across Africa, the Middle East and Asia** (WHO 2020). Most low- and middle-income countries (LMICs) have much **poorer health indices** than OECD countries (OECD 2021), and the WHO has estimated that countries with less than 23 health workers (doctors, nurses, midwives) per 10,000 population are **unable to deliver essential health services** (WHO 2016) … The loss of medical staff and resulting high levels of maternal and child mortality also has a **high economic cost** to the poorest countries … (Saluja et al. 2020).

Adapted from Eaton et al. (2023 p254) with bold added

 REFERENCING, UNDERSTANDING PLAGIARISM AND ETHICAL AI

Style 2: Focus on the *source*

In this writing style, you want the reader to be more aware of the authors/researchers (as well as their findings or ideas). Below is the same extract rewritten to show the change in emphasis. Here you naturally mention the author(s) names as part of the text. You add the year in brackets to pinpoint the sources listed in the reference list. You also need to use words to introduce the research – shown in bold.

Academic literature spanning decades, including **Beine, Doquier and Rapoport (2008)** and **Mills et al. (2008), has documented** the damage that the medical brain-drain does to health services in poorer countries. The **World Health Organisation (2020) draws attention** to the critical shortages of health workers across Africa, the Middle East and Asia. The **OECD (2021) shows** that most low- and middle-income countries (LMICs) have much poorer health indices than OECD countries. The **WHO has also estimated** that countries with less than 23 health workers (doctors, nurses, midwives) per 10,000 population are unable to deliver essential health services … **Saluja et al. (2020) argue** that the loss of medical staff and resulting high levels of maternal and child mortality also has a high economic cost to the poorest countries …

Adapted from Eaton et al. (2023 p254) with bold added

Your choice

When you write, use whichever style seems to fit most naturally in your sentences, and feel free to move between them in the same piece of writing.

The word-count factor

- Style 2 (focus on the source) is slightly longer than Style 1.
- Style 1 (focus on the ideas) is +10% longer than a numeric style (see Appendix A).

These figures may be inflated because we have used the extracts to illustrate points, but it is worth noting that numeric referencing styles are generally more economical with words.

Introducing sources

The language used to introduce the various studies and their authors in the Style 2 extract is active. The writers (Eaton et al.) are telling the reader what they think the authors are **doing** in the articles they report on.

Beine, Doquier and Rapoport (2008) and Mills et al. (2008), **have documented** … The World Health Organization (2020) **draws attention** to …The OECD (2021) **shows** that … Saluja et al. (2020) **argue** …

 REFERENCING, UNDERSTANDING PLAGIARISM AND ETHICAL AI

The choice of verb to introduce a study is a key strategy for indicating what you want to say about the source. It is satisfying to the reader (especially if it's your tutor!) to see from your choice of verb that YOU can see what authors are DOING in writing up their research.

Six magic verbs

Smith (2024)	points out argues maintains claims concludes suggests	that	preventative medicine is far more cost effective, and therefore better adapted to the developing world.

University of Manchester (2023). Academic Phasebank.
This is a tiny extract from this excellent resource for language to use in academic writing.

Try it!

Try using these words to introduce research into your work. You'll see how powerful they are in changing and shaping meaning. Use them to say what you mean. Use them carefully.

Using 'state' - don't!

Nicholson (2024) states that empowerment gives the employee the power and authority to do things at work.

All this tells your reader is that you have read Nicholson (probably) but you have absolutely nothing to say about it! It can lead to non committal 'descriptive' writing.

Only use when

… you present a statement by an author, often an organisation, which you then go on to discuss and examine:

Ofsted (2023) states that absence from school has been a 'stubborn problem' (px) since the pandemic. However, the question of how to address this …'

 REFERENCING, UNDERSTANDING PLAGIARISM AND ETHICAL AI

How sure are you?

Researchers are careful about their use of language when they write up their research:

Tentative	Definite
Emerging research	Established findings

When 'new knowledge' begins to emerge, researchers are cautious and tentative about their conclusions. They only make statements for which they feel the evidence is sound:

> *There is the possibility that …*
>
> *… findings also suggest that …*
>
> *Recent studies (…) indicate that …*

As knowledge in a field becomes more established, the debate moves on:

> *Dissenbak (2024) maintains …*
>
> *Two recent studies (Clogg and Klee 2023; Ballard 2025) challenge …*

And as 'knowledge' becomes confirmed by further studies, more categorical statements can be made

> *Konrad (2024) found / demonstrated / showed that …*

The key point here for you is:

DON'T OVERSTATE! Only be as definite in your language as the evidence allows you to be – and choose your words accordingly.

And if you want to show differences …?

If you want to show differences between the views and interpretations of experts in the field, or between an author's views and your own, your **choice of verb** can show how convinced you are by the views or findings of an author.

Try these!

Distant	Neutral	Close
Cohn (2023)		
claims that …		
discussed the idea …		
asserts …		
considers …		
contends …		
observed that …		
points out …		
reported …		
has shown …		
demonstrated …		
confirms that …		

 REFERENCING, UNDERSTANDING PLAGIARISM AND ETHICAL AI

Have something to say: use your topic sentences!

Using research in your writing isn't just about the techniques for referring to your sources – crucial though this is. It is about having something to say about what you've learnt; showing your line of reasoning, your position on something – your voice.

Look at how Alex used topic sentences to structure his argument (pp. 33–4).

2.1 Mobility cultures

The advent of mass motorisation across western civilisation had a major impact on cycling as an everyday method of transportation. In the UK cycling levels peaked in 1949 …

Alex's major point, his core argument, in the first topic sentence. It drives the whole section.

He starts to show his evidence that underpins this statement.

In the second half of the twentieth century, however, the pattern of cycling in mainland Europe and the UK diverged markedly…

The second major point in the topic sentence. Evidence follows.

No such change in attitudes to cycling took place in the UK. In the early 2000s, despite initiatives to broaden the appeal of cycling …

Third major point in the topic sentence (evidence follows).

This changed radically in the period of Covid-19 when restrictions and lockdowns led to a dramatic increase in cycling…

A marked change in focus in the topic sentence – the reader expects evidence to follow …

Regina too makes HER points in the topic sentence of each paragraph on the basis of the research she had done (pp63–4.).

The take-away point?

The topic sentence in each paragraph is where YOU make the statements you want to make. The evidence follows. This is the route to becoming a confident writer – with something to say.

UNDERSTANDING PLAGIARISM AND ETHICAL USE OF AI

Part 3 is designed to help you understand plagiarism so that you can avoid it, and to help you feel confident about how you can use AI.

Of course, some plagiarism is deliberate. Students who pay someone to do the work or blatantly cut and paste or copy others' work have not learnt anything. When they hand in work, they are claiming: 'Here's my assignment'. Quite plainly it isn't, and quite plainly this is cheating. This guide is not about that sort of plagiarism.

This guide is for students who do their own work and want to take credit for it but are worried that they don't understand plagiarism and might slip into it by accident. Part 3 explains what plagiarism is and how to make the right decisions to avoid it.

What is plagiarism?

There is no quick answer to this as there are many aspects to plagiarism. At university, plagiarism involves a set of steps:

A student

- takes something such as the work, words or ideas
- from someone else, such as an author of a journal article, a website, an organisation, another student, a family member – or even from your own work*
- as if it were their own work, or without making the source clear, or not making clear the distinction between their own work and others' work.

* See also explanation of self-plagiarism p83.

Good academic practice

Understanding good academic practice is just as important as understanding plagiarism: it's the other part of the picture. Just focusing on what you must not do does not necessarily guide you to what you need to do.

Good academic practice is about how you carry out your work from start to finish, step by step, by:

- really understanding the task before you start
- doing your research: from lecture notes, reading lists and independent research
- planning, constructing and preparing your assignment yourself
- drawing on sources from your notes (and some quotes, if needed)
- recording all references for in-text citations and the reference list (try using a reference manager / bibliographic software)
- citing sources in your text in the right place so your links are clear
- writing the assignment in your own words.

All this is hard work! If you use AI in any of the above, make sure you are using it as a tool to help you – not taking your place as author.

Many courses require students to sign a sheet saying the work is their own. You must have ticked dozens of boxes on websites to say you've read the terms and conditions (really?). But what are you signing up to when you sign: 'This is my work'?

WORK not words!

We are talking about WORK here, not just about words. Parts 1 and 2 describe some of the work involved in writing good assignments: identifying sources, taking notes, linking your sources with your points and arguments ... for starters. Then there's the work of turning your ideas into words and the work of putting the whole thing together as a cogent piece of text. All that most definitely adds up to WORK!

 REFERENCING, UNDERSTANDING PLAGIARISM AND ETHICAL AI

This is what you are being assessed on. This is what you take credit for – and this is a major route by which you learn.

Is this my work?

If you use AI, ask yourself the following checklist questions before you submit any work:

- ☐ Am I the author?
- ☐ Is it right for me to put my name to this?
- ☐ Do I want to put my name to this?
- ☐ Is it me talking in this text?
- ☐ Would I be able to answer questions on what I am submitting?
- ☐ Have I met the learning outcomes for this task?
- ☐ Have I followed instructions on appropriate use of AI for this assignment and at my institution?

Learning: the point of it all

Tutors design courses, assignments and 'learning experiences' which they think will promote learning. They also have to make sure that the rules are followed and that anyone who gets credit for achieving something does so by the rules and plays fair.

The 'rules of the university game' might be explained like this:

We don't give credit for students doing the assignment. We give credit if students learn something by doing the work we set.

Learning is also the point of it all for you. Think of the purpose of your course for you, your development and your future working life. If you are doing your course without learning, then you are missing these opportunities.

What's the difference?

Look at this table to see the difference.

A student hands in an assignment that shows ...	What's going on?
'I took care of seven people with emphysema.'	That's doing something OK, but that's all it is.
'I took care of seven patients with emphysema and here is a care plan about the best ways to take care of patients with emphysema which I found in my textbook.'	That's not learning, that's doing something and copying. And they don't connect. Is the care any better for having read the textbook? There's no evidence of it.

 REFERENCING, UNDERSTANDING PLAGIARISM AND ETHICAL AI

> | |
> | --- |
> | *'Two months ago, I could not have made a care plan for a patient with emphysema. Now I have taken care of seven, done some reading and talked with people who know about it and, now, here's my care plan.'* | That's learning, and the plan shows the work that went into the learning. It is based on the evidence of other people's work in the field, informing your own ideas and approach. |

In this last example you are **applying** what you learnt. You can only do this when you fully understand, have thought about it and relate it to your own circumstance. 'Applying' is near the top of the 'stairway to critical thinking'.

See p47 (stairway) and *Getting Critical* in this series

Note on self-plagiarism

You need to be clear when you can and cannot use your own work a second time. Self-plagiarism is taking your own work, that you previously submitted for credit, and reusing it (all or parts) to submit for credit another time.

This is not about drafts of work you produce on the way to a final piece, or early work that feeds into later submissions (both completely acceptable and expected), but where you reuse a previously submitted assignment for a different course or module when you should be submitting new work.

You can only get credit for a piece of work once!

When you first start working on an assignment, you may be thinking: It has to be 'my own work'. Does that mean no one can help?

No. You can and should ask others for help and advice when you need it. But what kind of help is acceptable?

Here's a simple test about asking for advice: Are you asking for advice or help so **you** can do the work? Or do it better? If the answer is 'yes', then that's fine.

Or is the 'help' really about getting someone else to **do the work for you**? This is not OK.

DO ask tutors or university study advisers for advice
Don't hesitate! Just ask – it's what they are there for.
Getting advice early on is always a good idea – it kick-starts your understanding of what the assignment is asking you to do, and can help you with planning your work.

What other sorts of help can you use?

1 Help with looking for sources

YES	NO
▸ When someone shows you how to locate sources or use databases. ▸ If using others' research to trigger your own: for example, tracking down the references from another source.	▸ If it means someone else doing the searching and choosing for you.

2 Help with writing citations and references

YES	NO
▸ If you are checking against available guides and trying to format correctly. ▸ If you are choosing the references for the assignment yourself.	▸ If you are relying on referencing tools, including AI, to do your research and choose the sources for you.

3 Consulting classmates about your work

YES

- Discussion is a great way to shape your own ideas. If you are *not* talking to people about your subject, you are really missing out!
- And especially yes when discussion sends you back to do more thinking and research.

NO

- If you just swallow other people's ideas and copy them as if they were yours ('without attribution').
- Sharing files of work with classmates – this is an invitation to copy and will land both the sender and receiver in trouble.

 REFERENCING, UNDERSTANDING PLAGIARISM AND ETHICAL AI

4 Using AI as a personal tutor

YES, for	NO, if you
<li> brainstorming ideas to build on<li> explaining key words<li> teaching you new concepts or methods<li> testing your knowledge on a topic<li> giving you feedback to help you improve your work.	<li> use AI to write or rewrite your assignment<li> rely on guidance from AI, instead of checking with your human tutor or assignment instructions.

Getting help with writing

A huge range of websites and tools, especially AI tools, are available to help with academic writing, so you need to make good decisions about the use of these tools. Think about the following:

Using AI tools for paraphrasing

YES, if	NO, if you
▶ you are using AI to paraphrase some words, phrases or a short section of text. Check that the paraphrase makes sense. ▶ it reflects what you want to say: you are still the author taking responsibility for the text.	▶ are getting AI to do a complete paraphrase of your whole text or large sections of it. ▶ allow AI to become the author. It can only be a tool you use to help you.

Example: ChatGPT

We uploaded the sentences below adapted from Henderson (2025) *Using AI to track down leftovers.*

Source text (adapted from Henderson, 2025)
Globally, an estimated one-fifth of food produced for human consumption is lost or wasted, which equals one billion meals every single day. Pioneering AI use could reduce that huge waste.

 REFERENCING, UNDERSTANDING PLAGIARISM AND ETHICAL AI

Paraphrase using ChatGPT-4o	Comments
Prompt: paraphrase so most of the words are different Around the world, roughly 20% of food intended for people ends up discarded or unused — the equivalent of a billion meals daily. Innovative applications of artificial intelligence may help curb this massive loss.	▸ This version sounds more vague. ▸ AI tools often overuse em dash — ▸ Some words are quite complex eg 'discarded' and 'curb'

Using AI and other tools for plagiarism checking

Of the many plagiarism checking tools available now, Turnitin is the one used by most universities (see Chapter 10), but students often want to find a way to check plagiarism online themselves:

YES	NO
▸ Use Turnitin and get advice on use of sources from your tutor (see Chapter 10).	▸ Don't upload your work to online plagiarism or checking tools. The check may be inaccurate and the site may make use of your assignment.

Using AI tools for translation

You can translate source material from one language to another very easily using AI tools or Google Translate.

YES	NO
▶ If you check with your tutor who agrees you may use some sources in translation (properly cited and translated).	▶ **If you use texts in other languages** and translate them without citing, or without making clear what is your own work and what is work by other authors.
▶ If you use AI tools to translate words, phrases or small sections of text.	▶ **If you use AI tools to translate** the whole text or large sections of it, from one language to another. In this case, you are no longer the author of the text.
▶ If you check AI outputs carefully before using.	▶ **If you use a translation tool without checking** the accuracy of the output. AI or digital tools for translation tools might change the original text by introducing a bias (such as gender or ethnicity).

Example: Google Translate

Source text
Globally, an estimated one-fifth of food produced for human consumption is lost or wasted, which equals one billion meals every single day. Pioneering AI use could reduce that huge waste.

Translation (Spanish)	Comments
A nivel mundial, se estima que una quinta parte de los alimentos producidos para el consumo humano se pierde o se desperdicia, lo que equivale a mil millones de comidas cada día. El uso pionero de la inteligencia artificial podría reducir ese enorme desperdicio.	Check the translation ▸ is accurate. ▸ reflects what you want to say. Always do some back translations and check the meaning of individual words.

Using AI tools for language correction or improvement

AI is commonly used by students to proofread their work, particularly to check grammar, spelling or academic style.

<table>
<tr><th>YES</th><th>NO</th></tr>
<tr><td>

- Check for grammar and spelling errors.
- Make some improvements to academic style.
- Use as an assistive tool to help you to develop your work.

</td><td>

- If you use AI to completely edit and rewrite your work so that you are no longer the author of the text.

</td></tr>
</table>

Example: Grammarly

We uploaded the student text below, which contains a number of spelling and grammatical errors, to a widely used AI tool.

Student text

I experience significant personal and academic development through working on my project and completing the weekly logboos. Both takes have helped me reflecting deeply on my strength and weaknessas a student. This esasay explores what I learned from the process. My initinal interest came from my bussiness experience, where I withnessed how fragial supply chains can be especially in pedemic. I knew litter about the topic, but I deeply impressed by a PLT process where captured caron dioxied and hydrygen are connected in clean aviatin fuel. Sturtuing was not easy. I added too much information and look clear topic sentence. After several themaditly, write more focused and creat better trainsation.

<table>
<tr><td>

AI Tool: Grammarly

I have experienced significant personal and academic development through working on my project and completing the weekly logbooks. Both tasks have helped me reflect deeply on my strengths and weaknesses as a student. This essay explores what I learned from the process.

My initial interest stemmed from my business experience, where I witnessed how fragile supply chains can be, especially during a pandemic. I knew little about the topic, but I was deeply impressed by a process in which captured carbon dioxide and hydrogen are used to create clean aviation fuel.

</td><td>

Comments

▶ Grammar and spelling corrected.

▶ Paragraphs created.

</td></tr>
</table>

Writing was not easy. I included too much information and lost the clarity of my main topic sentence. After several revisions, I was able to focus more and create better transitions.	<ul><li>Revision of final part seems to have been made through guessed content.</li><li>Some changes made to meaning eg 'lost the clarity'.</li><li>'themaditly' has been changed to 'revisions'</li><li>'write more focused' is quite different as 'I was able to focus more' (does not mention writing)</li></ul>

So, AI tools might help you gain awareness of spelling and grammatical errors. That's good! Then you can correct them. But if you use them simply to make your work better, without any effort from you, then you are not doing your own work. Be an active learner and keep improving yourself!

AI is likely to be embedded in any application you are using, which makes it more difficult to take responsibility. When you are using any computer application, always check you are in control and making the decisions about what you use, rather than leaving it to AI.

 REFERENCING, UNDERSTANDING PLAGIARISM AND ETHICAL AI

Deceptive use of AI

If you hide your use of AI, and pretend that AI outputs are your own work, this is obviously not ethical. You should be transparent about use of AI by:

- declaring it according to your institution's system (eg a declaration form, a cover sheet, an acknowledgements section)
- ensuring it is in line with your assignment instructions.

Help from essay writing tools

There are a huge number of essay writing sites which offer to write your essay for you. They also suggest they can 'help' you write.

NO! Only NO for this one. This is not your work! Universities take a very strong line against these sites which compromise the authenticity of student work. In some countries, including within the UK, these sites are illegal. Don't use these websites for anything. They may have free essays or samples available or offer you 'tutorials' to help with your work, but any use of these websites is likely to lead to problems. Keep away!

Think about where you draw the line between acceptable practices and plagiarism. Read the following extract and assess how it is used in the quiz below.

Using AI to track down leftovers

Globally, an estimated one-fifth of food produced for human consumption is lost or wasted, which equals one billion meals every single day. Pioneering AI use could reduce that huge waste.

The problem isn't only what actually goes into the bin though. There is also the issue of food loss in which deterioration or loss during transportation, lack of refrigeration, etc., prevents products from reaching our plates at all. Food loss and waste affect not only food prices, but also the energy used to grow, process, distribute and cook the food. And it doesn't end there. Much of this wasted food ends up in landfill without the right conditions to properly decompose. Starved of oxygen, it rots anaerobically creating methane, which once in the atmosphere is 80 times more potent at warming than carbon dioxide.

 REFERENCING, UNDERSTANDING PLAGIARISM AND ETHICAL AI

Vijay Nair and his team in culinary operations at the University of Guelph, Canada had previously tracked food waste using time-consuming manual methods of using pen, paper and spreadsheets. But since November 2024, in one of the university's prep kitchens he's been using Winnow, software by a British AI solution company that uses data analysis to reduce food waste in commercial kitchens. The tool, currently used in more than 40 universities around the world, consists of a small terminal with a camera inside that's fitted over a normal kitchen bin and has a set of scales beneath it. Thanks to the data provided by AI, kitchen managers can anticipate and adapt their purchase orders and menus. "Considering that, by value, nearly 70 per cent of wasted food is wasted before it gets to the customer or the student, this is crucial," says David Jackson from Winnow. The company aims to cut food waste in half in 12 to 24 months.

Adapted from Henderson, E. (2025). Using AI to track down leftovers. *UNESCO Courier*, 2/4/25. Available at: https://courier.unesco.org/en/articles/using-ai-track-down-leftovers

Quiz: Where do you draw the line?

Four student writers used the text above in an essay on the use of AI as a solution to environmental problems. Decide for each whether the use is the right side or the wrong side of the line between good academic writing and leaning too heavily on someone else's work.

1	Food loss occurs through deterioration during transportation and lack of refrigeration, which prevent products from reaching our plates at all. Food loss and waste affect not only food prices, but also the energy used to grow, process, distribute and cook the food. Much of this wasted food ends up in landfill without the right conditions to properly decompose. Starved of oxygen, it rots anaerobically creating methane, which once in the atmosphere is 80 times more potent at warming than carbon dioxide. Globally, an estimated one-fifth of food produced for human consumption is lost or wasted, which equals one billion meals every single day. Pioneering AI use could reduce that huge waste. The company aims to cut food waste in half in 12 to 24 months. (Henderson, 2025)
2	Henderson (2025) explains the food waste problem. They first demonstrate how the problems of food loss and food waste are caused and explain that food loss and waste affect not only food prices, but also the energy used to grow, process, distribute and cook the food. Because the food waste is starved of oxygen, it rots anaerobically creating methane, which once in the atmosphere is 80 times more potent at warming than carbon dioxide.
3	Henderson (2025) presents an AI solution to the global problem of food loss and food waste, which has reached one billion meals per day. A new AI company uses a camera and scales to measure waste in the food bin and 'the company aims to cut food waste in half in 12 to 24 months'.

 REFERENCING, UNDERSTANDING PLAGIARISM AND ETHICAL AI

| 4 | Henderson (2025) explores the potential for an AI tool to help reduce food waste. First, the author explains how the problems of food loss and food waste occur, and why they are so significant. Then they explain a case where a new AI tool measures the waste using a camera and scales to enable kitchen managers to adapt their orders and reduce waste; the company goal is to reduce waste by 50% within one to two years. |

See next page for our comments on the examples above. They are presented upside down.

1	This is just copy and paste. Although the writer has chosen sentences from different parts of the text, they are copied word for word, so this is clearly plagiarism and does not show any learning.
2	This writer starts by citing the article to start creating their own message, which is good, but then falls back on too much copying. The reader will definitely notice complex words like 'anaerobically' and will start to wonder whose work this is.
3	This writer makes a good effort to use the text by starting with a clear topic sentence which summarises the main point. The quote, however, does not seem necessary as the information could easily be paraphrased. Words need to be special for a quote (see p51) and the writer should always comment on it. Despite its faults, this writing is acceptable.
4	This is an effective summary of all of the key points, reformulated and in a different order, showing an understanding of the message of the source text. It's a good piece of writing.

10   Use of Turnitin

Turnitin, the electronic text-matching tool, is used by most universities worldwide. Understanding plagiarism at university includes understanding some things about Turnitin.

What can you see on Turnitin?

- Coloured matches to uses of the same words in the same order as other texts.
- Calculations of percentages representing how much of the submitted work can be matched to other texts (overall amount and breakdown of individual matches).

The extracts below show some matching of a source text by Turnitin.

Example 1: Low Transport Neighbourhoods

feedback studio

In this paper, the term 'LTNs' will be used to refer to the general concept of an area with restricted motor vehicle traffic. In addition, the term 'traffic congestion' will be used to refer to the many vehicles, overfilled capacity, or uncoordinated traffic flow, and the term 'liveable urban environments' will be used to specify the urban spaces designed to prioritize the well-being and quality of life of residents.

Do the matches mean plagiarism?

No, the matches do not necessarily mean plagiarism. They mean that the submission has similarities to other texts. If the use of these texts is properly cited, with appropriate quotation formatting where necessary, and references given, then it is not plagiarism. Too much textual similarity may indicate a problem of overr-eliance on other sources,

 **REFERENCING, UNDERSTANDING PLAGIARISM AND ETHICAL AI**

but this is not plagiarism if the above conditions are met. In addition, many matches are expected such as to academic phrases, task titles, institutional addresses, reference lists – these examples don't need citing.

Example 1 above shows a match to a well-used phrase 'in this paper, the term … will be used to refer to'. These words don't belong to anyone and do not have any content-specific information, so they do not need to be cited. Matches like this are not plagiarism – they are good practice!

Example 2: Use of AI by the fashion industry

Turnitin highlights matched text with gaps, including a citation within the match.

The partnership intends to develop an "enterprise data backbone" which includes "a core data platform" which uses AI (Gray, 2022). H&M has an integrated AI department with over 250 data scientists writing algorithms from loyalty cards, online purchases, store receipts, and product returns to forecast trends and future purchases (Chaudhuri, 2018). The company has also established an AI driven initiative, Body Scan Jeans for an enhanced customer experience, The initiative allows H&M to deliver personalized clothing adapting to the needs of the consumer with the help of AI (Kaplan, 2024).

Matches on Turnitin do indicate plagiarism if larger sections of text (two or more sentences) have been copied without citation or '…' (quotation marks). Inadequate paraphrasing can also show up on Turnitin and could be considered plagiarism where the student's text is too similar to the source text.

Even where there isn't a continuous match, Turnitin shows up strings of words with gaps. In Example 2, some strings of words are matched to the same source over two sentences: 'from loyalty cards … H&M to …'. This would be considered inadequate paraphrasing as the writer is relying on source text for most of the sentences.

Part of the match is to a citation, (Chaudhuri, 2018). It appears that the student has copied directly from another source where this citation was used, presenting another author's reading and interpretation, not their own. This is very poor practice.

Example 3: Sustainable aviation fuel

feedback studio

6. References

Ansell, P.J. (2023) 'Review of sustainable energy carriers for aviation: Benefits, challenges, and future viability', *Progress in Aerospace Sciences*, 141, article number 100919. Available at: https://doi.org/10.1016/j.paerosci.2023.100919

Biermann, F. and Pattberg, P. (2008) 'Global environmental governance: Taking stock, moving forward', *Annual Review of Environment and Resources*, 33(1), pp. 277-294. Available at: https://www.researchgate.net/publication/228203186_Global_Environmental_Governance_Taking_Stock_Moving_Forward

Borrill, E., Koh, S.L. and Yuan, R. (2024) 'Review of technological developments and LCA applications on biobased SAF conversion processes', *Frontiers in Fuels*, 2, article number 1397962. Available at: https://doi.org/10.3389/ffuel.2024.1397962

Breuer, J.L., Scholten, J., Koj, J.C., Schorn, F., Fiebrandt, M., Samsun, R.C., Albus, R., Görner, K., Stolten, D. and Peters, R. (2022) 'An overview of promising alternative fuels for road, rail, air, and inland waterway transport in Germany', *Energies*, 15(4), article number 1443. Available at: https://doi.org/10.3390/en15041443

If you have matches to your reference list, that's great because it shows you are using known, genuine sources (not fabricated by AI or anyone). The reader can see that if they click on the DOI or URL, they will be able to go directly to the source.

What should you do about the matches?

Discuss with a tutor or adviser and make sure you fully understand about how you are using sources, what mistakes you may be making, what you need to revise and what you can leave as it is.

Do NOT get the idea that you need to 'make the colour go away'. Matches can indicate both good practice and plagiarism, so you need to make sure you distinguish between matches to change and matches to leave.

Apart from Turnitin

Your reader has other means of telling if it is your work:

- **style changes**: the language used by student writers, published writers and random web sources is usually quite different
- **mix of referencing systems**: some numeric, some author-date, some with no references at all, or unusual references

 REFERENCING, UNDERSTANDING PLAGIARISM AND ETHICAL AI

- **oddities in expertise**: when a complicated problem, say, or very advanced methodology is dropped into a piece of work without explanation.

What to remember about plagiarism

Use **'I am doing my own work'** as your guiding principle to decide what is OK and what is not OK when you are writing assignments.

- **It is OK** when you are actively engaged in researching, preparing, structuring, citing, paraphrasing, summarising and writing your assignment.
- **It is not OK** when you are not actively engaged because you are borrowing too much from other authors or you are getting others, or other tools including AI, to do your work for you.

REFERENCING: THE PRACTICALITIES

Part 4 starts with answers to **frequently asked questions** about referencing (Chapter 11). Chapter 12 gives **examples and guidelines** for how to reference **essential sources:** books, journal articles, online materials, social media sources and more.

Examples show how to cite the source in your text and list it in your reference list.

References or bibliography? What's the difference?

In Harvard and many other referencing styles (see Appendix) the **Reference list** or **'References'** is a list of all the sources you have referred to in your writing. This is what most tutors require.

A **bibliography** is a list of everything you have read on a subject, including background reading, whether you refer to it or not. You may occasionally be asked for a bibliography (of your reading to date): for example when your tutor wants to see where you have got to in your research for a dissertation proposal.

If you are asked for a bibliography for a finished piece of work, divide it into two sections:

1 *References:* for sources you cite in your text
2 *Other sources consulted:* for materials you have read but chose not to use.

Tutors sometimes use the term 'Bibliography' to mean 'Reading list' or 'Suggested reading'.

Some referencing styles (including MHRA, Chicago (Notes and Bibliography), MLA and Oscola) refer to the list of 'references' at the end of a piece of work as a 'bibliography'. This often lists all the sources you cite in footnotes and endnotes, pulling it all together in one list (see Appendix B)

How do I reference a source I found in a book/article but I haven't actually read it myself?

The answer is simple. You only list something in your references if **you have actually read that source**. You list the text where *you* found it in your references list, and refer to the actual source in your work. This is called **secondary referencing**.

In your work	Reference list
Hertzberg (1959) identified two different sets of factors affecting motivation and work (Hertzberg, Mausner and Synderman 1959, cited in Mullins 2023 p242), described as the 'two-factor' theory of …	Mullins LJ and Rees G (2023). *Management and organisational behaviour* 13th edn. UK: Pearson Education.

In this example, you haven't read Herzberg et al., but you have read the chapter in Mullins, your textbook, which summarises and discusses Herzberg et al.'s theory. You cite Herzberg et al. in your text (with page numbers) and point your reader to where you found it (Mullins) – so they can find it too.

> **Using sources you haven't read yourself**
>
> Not a good idea. At best you're relying on someone else's summary or account of something. At worst the source has been fabricated by AI and the research is entirely fake.

A primary source is information collected and written up by the organisation or person who carried out the work at first hand: data collection, a case study, observations, theory, analysis.

Secondary sources are written by someone who has read the primary source and described it in some way. A textbook is a secondary source that includes a lot of references to primary sources. An article may review other research (so here it's a secondary source) before going on to report on the authors' own primary research.

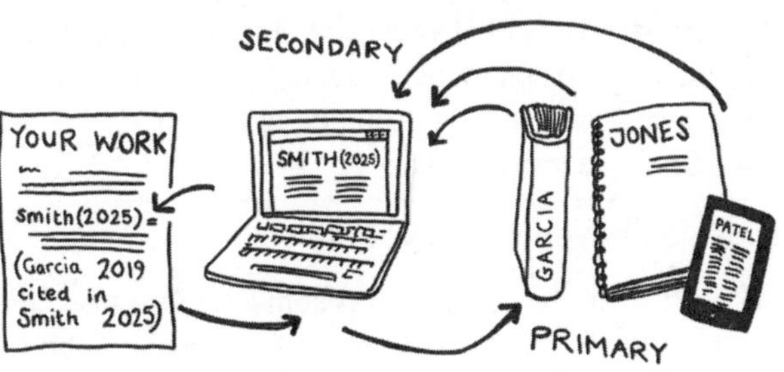

Tertiary sources are collections or summaries of other sources: encyclopaedias, directories, dictionaries, Wikipedia. They are useful to orientate you on a topic but not close enough to the original primary research to be useful as evidence in your writing.

Use primary sources wherever you can, and be careful about relying too heavily on secondary sources. A textbook or article that summarises a lot of work in the field is a good place to start for an overview. However, if you don't go and find the actual sources, your understanding of the study, data or whatever is limited to the short summary you find in the textbook. You may then have to paraphrase someone else's summary. If you do this a lot, it will be clear to your reader that you have only read the one textbook and this is the only one you can list in your references.

However, when the original is hard to find (eg it is old, or has restricted circulation) and you want to use it because it is special in some way, do so as in the boxed Hertzberg example on p109.

When do I put in page numbers?

If what you are referring to came from a specific page, then give the page number if available.

Look for the page number for
▶ any quote
▶ any figure or illustration you refer to.

If you are referring to a general idea, or summarising a whole section or chunk, then don't give the page number(s) – your reader will need to read more to understand the material.

Online articles may not have page numbers – they start from p1. If there is a pdf version, check if there is a page number.

Why do authors put in a string of references?

You are most likely to see a string of references at the beginning of an article. The authors may want to refer briefly to **well-established research findings**, and then to move on swiftly to the issues that concern them. Note that the extracts below order their citations differently.

Citations are usually given in date order by year of publication (oldest first), as here: it implies a **history** in the development of a topic.

> Cycling levels vary widely between countries and many factors have been identified, including cycling infrastructure, gender and age (Pucher and Beuhler 2012; Mueller et al. 2018; Aldred and Goodman 2019).

Or the author/s may want to give an overview of research on **different aspects** of the topic and cite their sources by alphabetical order of author.

> Some studies of children's reading found better reading comprehension on screens than on paper, whereas others found no difference between the media (Halamish and Elbaz 2019; Hermena et al. 2017; Lenhard, Schroeders and Lenhard 2017; Singer and Alexander 2016).

In reality, tutors are unlikely to be looking for this level of detail and both styles are perfectly correct.

For more on grouping references, see *Doing your Literature Review* in this series.

 REFERENCING, UNDERSTANDING PLAGIARISM AND ETHICAL AI

> **Being credited as an author matters to researchers**
> especially in relation to the number of **citations** in other publications – research articles, reviews, policy documents. It is an indicator of contribution to the field.
> At the time of writing (late 2025), the article by Eaton et al. had 19 citations in peer-reviewed journal articles and five in policy documents. These broader measures of impact are reflected in various '**Citation metrics**'.
>
> Given the time it takes between writing and publication, the article seems to be making a useful contribution to this research area – a useful point for you, as a researcher, to notice.

What if the same author has several publications in the same year?

When you want to refer to several articles or documents by the same author all published in the same year, you need to be able to show your reader which is which. This most often happens with a:

- weekly journal or newspaper when a journalist writes regularly on the same or similar topics
- government or official body that issues statements, guidelines, reports or policies on a regular basis.

In your work	Reference list
You show which is which by adding a letter to the year: The pressures on international expenditure on different aspects of health is well documented (OECD 2023b) with …	OECD (2023a) (+full details). Organisation for Economic Cooperation and Development (2023b). *Understanding international measures* of health spending. Available at: https://doi.org/10.1787/043ed664-en (Accessed 30 June 2025) OECD (2023c) + (full details)

When do I use 'et al.'?

'Et al.' is a shortening of the Latin *'et alia'* which means 'and others'. It is used in referencing when there are multiple authors, more than is sensible to write out in your text, or even in your reference list.

'et al.' Author/date (Harvard) style	
In your work	**Reference list**
Use 'et al.' with four or more authors.	List all authors. References can be listed in alphabetical order by name of first author, or in order of seniority in the research team.
Eaton et al. (2023) argue that the brain drain of health staff from poorer to richer countries can only be addressed by richer countries training their own workforces.	Eaton J, Baingana F, Abdulaziz M, Obindo T, Skuse D, Jenkins R (2023). The negative impact of global health worker migration, and how it can be addressed. *Public Health*. 225, Dec 2023, pp254–257. Available at: https://doi.org/10.1016/j.puhe.2023.09.014

Harvard has no single authoritative handbook, so advice varies. Our advice credits all authors with their contribution, from the first named, the lead author (often an eminent professor), to the last, a researcher, perhaps a PhD student.

Give each reference a sequential number starting from 1. Keep the same number for that source every time you use it. Use 'et al.' for six or more authors.

If you use a source near the beginning of your work,[3] and again later in the assignment after several other references,[3, 12,15] it keeps its number – the full details of the reference are only listed once.

The authors listed below are the first six in a big team of 16 researchers – not all their names are given even in the reference. They are, however, listed in full in the article itself.

In your work	Reference list
	Listed in number order of first use.
Pay and security have been key drivers of healthcare workers' migration,[16] but career prospects and job satisfaction are also significant[12, 15] …	16 Toyin-Thomas P, Ikhurionan P, Omoyibo, EE, Iwegim C, Ukueku AO, Okpere J, et al. Drivers of health workers' migration, intention to migrate and non-migration from low/middle-income countries, 1970–2022: a systematic review. *BMJ Global Health*. 8 (2023). Article e012338.
The article number can be helpful in locating an article where no doi is given.	

Critical thinking – the strategic questions

Look back to the strategic questions (p. 9), and see how they can be useful to you here.

The team of researchers in the example above includes experts from across continents – universities and hospitals in Canada, Nigeria and the US. Their purpose is to mount and evidence a persuasive argument: the profile and status of the authors strengthens this.

> **Who** wrote it?
>
> **How** are they qualified?
>
> **What** is their expertise?
>
> **How valid** is their evidence?
>
> **So how might I use** this source?

Thinking about the expertise of authors is, of course, an important element in your critical evaluation of your reading. Good referencing is a key step in becoming a reflective and 'critical' researcher and writer.

This chapter gives examples of references from a range of frequently used sources: online sources, books and journal articles and suggests an approach for referencing the unexpected.

How to reference a book

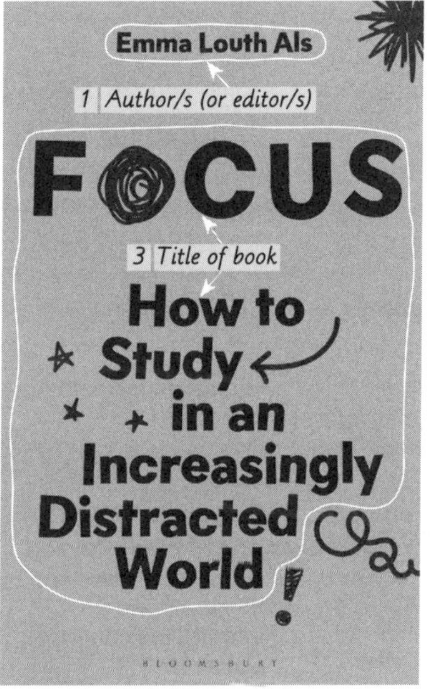

The six points of a book (or ebook) reference

1 **Author**(s) or **editor**(s) as shown on the title page: family name/surname first, followed by initial(s)
2 **Year** of publication (in brackets). Give the date of the edition you are using
3 **Title** of the book in *italics*
4 **Edition** (if not first)
5 **Place of publication** – traditional, widely used, but no longer always required
6 **Publisher**

Books can be written by individuals. Organisations can also be the author.

Book references

In your work (one author)	Reference list
Louth Als (2026 p78) offers a checklist for recognising addiction to social media …	Louth Als E (2026). *Focus: How to study in an increasingly distracted world*. Bloomsbury.

This is a short reference with a single author: it's a first edition, so no need to give Edition number (4), and we have chosen not to include Place of publication (5).

 REFERENCING, UNDERSTANDING PLAGIARISM AND ETHICAL AI

Two authors	Reference list
By 1928 the world's population was about 2 billion. Then the rate of increase rose rapidly to 2.5 billion in 1968, rising to 5 billion by 1987 and 7.7 billion by 2019 (Kidder and May 2022). Since then …	Kidder J and May E (2022). *Climate Change* for Dummies. Newark: John Wiley and Sons.
Three authors	
The onset of sickle cell disease is vividly portrayed in the 'clinical case' introducing Chapter 19 Blood (Martini, Nath and Bartholomew 2023 p686). Symptoms include …	Martini F, Nath JL and Bartholomew EF (2023). *Fundamentals of anatomy and physiology.* 12th edn / Global edition. Harlow, Essex: Pearson.
Four or more authors	
The report notes that 'a significant proportion' of government support for food and agriculture is counterproductive (Food and Agriculture Organization of the United Nations et al. (2022 pvi). It distorts market prices, is environmentally destructive and fails to deliver a healthy diet for children.	Food and Agriculture Organization of the United Nations et al. (2022). *The state of food security and nutrition in the world 2022: Repurposing food and agricultural policies to make healthy diets more affordable.* Rome: FAO. This report is also available at: https://openknowledge.fao.org/server/api/core/bitstreams/67b1e9c7-1a7f-4dc6-a19e-f6472a4ea83a/content (Accessed 15 July 2025)

A chapter in an edited book

In your work you refer to the author(s) of the chapter you are using. Your reader looks for this name in your references, and sees the book (or eBook) it is in.

In your work	Reference list
The case study used by Ogden (2022 p141) suggests that beliefs about food and the individual's experience of eating are powerful factors in …	Ogden J (2022). Health psychology. In J Naidoo and J Wills (eds). *Health studies: an introduction* (4th edn). Bloomsbury. pp118–143.

eBooks

When an eBook looks like a printed book, and has all the details of a printed book, reference it like a printed book (as in the example above). If you find the reference to the book in an electronic format (you might be reading this in our eBook version, for example), it is convenient to be able to go to the source with a click. In a big eBook each chapter may have its own doi.

To access eBooks held by your institution's library (Oxford Brookes University in the example below) you go in via the library portal.

In your work	Reference list
Andrews (2020) starts her exploration of the animal mind by discussing the ways to investigate …	Andrews K (2020). *The animal mind: an introduction to the philosophy of animal cognition* (2nd edn). Routledge. Available at: https://doi-org.oxfordbrookes.idm.oclc.org/10.4324/9780203712511

If you don't have access to a college or university library, you may be able to find an open-access online library.

How to reference a journal article

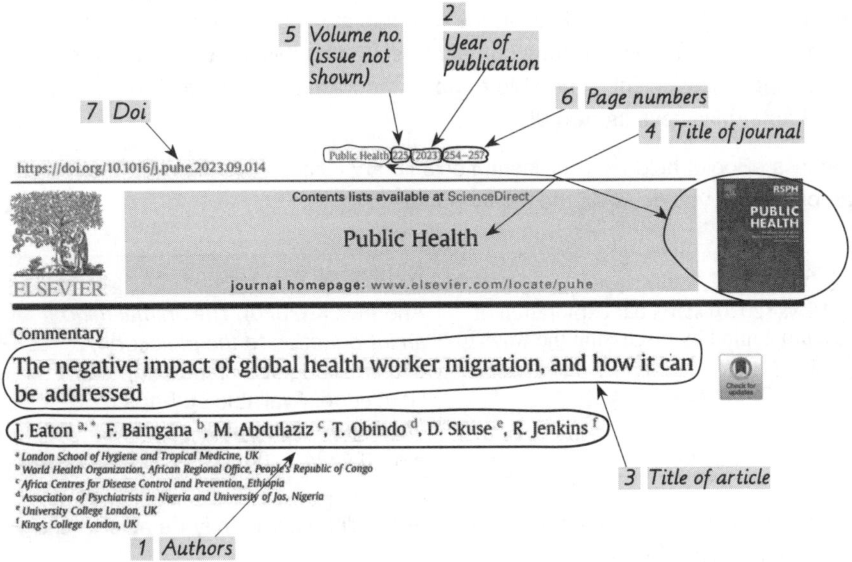

https://doi.org/10.1016/j.puhe.2023.09.014

Public Health 225 (2023) 254–257

Contents lists available at ScienceDirect

Public Health

journal homepage: www.elsevier.com/locate/puhe

ELSEVIER

PUBLIC HEALTH

Commentary

The negative impact of global health worker migration, and how it can be addressed

J. Eaton [a, *], F. Baingana [b], M. Abdulaziz [c], T. Obindo [d], D. Skuse [e], R. Jenkins [f]

[a] London School of Hygiene and Tropical Medicine, UK
[b] World Health Organization, African Regional Office, People's Republic of Congo
[c] Africa Centres for Disease Control and Prevention, Ethiopia
[d] Association of Psychiatrists in Nigeria and University of Jos, Nigeria
[e] University College London, UK
[f] King's College London, UK

<table>
<tr><td colspan="2">The seven points of a journal reference</td></tr>
<tr><td colspan="2">

1 **Author**(s) in the order shown: family name/surname first, followed by initial(s)
2 **Year** of publication (in brackets)
3 **Full title of article**
4 **Title of journal** in *italics*
5 **Details**: volume/issue/month (if shown)
6 **Pages** of the article (if shown)
7 **Available at**: https:**//doi.**org... (Digital Object Identifier)

If there is no doi, use:
Available at [URL] (Accessed + date)

</td></tr>
</table>

With the DOI you can find the article with a click – and satisfy yourself that it is a genuine human-authored source, not fabricated by AI.

In your work	Reference list
Eaton et al. (2023) argue that the solution to the migration of trained healthcare staff from poor countries to richer countries is to increase the number of medical and nursing students trained in the UK.	Eaton J, Baingana F, Abdulaziz M, Obindo T, Skuse D, Jenkins R. (2023). The negative impact of global health worker migration, and how it can be addressed. *Public Health*. 225 Dec pp254–257. Available at: https://doi.org/10.1016/j.puhe.2023.09.014

For referencing purposes, there is no distinction between online journal articles (that only exist online) and journal articles that exist in print but you find online.

The question for you is whether the article has a doi or not:

- Where an article has a doi, you can find it with (Ctrl + click) or pasting the doi into a database or search engine. The details 'Available at [URL] (Accessed + date)' are not relevant or needed.
- Where there is no doi, show the route you took: Available at [URL] (Accessed + date).

In your work	Reference list
One author	
Fitness apps via mobile devices (eg smartphones and wrist-worn wearables) have become a 'central source of fitness and health' (Kim 2022). The study …	Kim HM (2022). Social comparison of fitness social media postings by fitness app users. *Computers in Human Behavior*. 131(3). June. Available at: https://doi.org/10.1016/j.chb.2022.107204
Two authors	
Asongu and Odhiambo (2019) conclude that mobile banking apps make positive contribution to addressing poverty and inequality in developing countries.	Asongu SA and Odhiambo NM (2019). Mobile banking usage, quality of growth, inequality and poverty in developing countries. *Information development*. 35(2). Available at: https://doi.org/10.1177/0266666917744006
This journal is online only: the reference shows the volume and issue of the journal but not the pages.	

Three authors	
In the area of reading and technology, the findings suggest that girls read more online, reflecting their tendency to read more in print (Loh, Sun and Majid 2020).	Loh CE, Sun B and Majid S (2019). Do girls read differently from boys? Adolescents and their gendered reading habits and preferences. *English in Education*. 54(2) pp174–190. Available at: https://doi.org/10.1080/04250494.2019.1610328
Four or more authors	
In their study of intra-generational differences among generation Z employees, Leslie et al. (2021) identified three distinct subgroups: Social Investors, Chill Worker Bees, and Go Getters …	Leslie B, Anderson C, Bickham C, Horman J, Overly A, Gentry C, Callahan C and King J (2021). Generation Z Perceptions of a Positive Workplace Environment. *Employee Responsibility and Rights Journal*. 33 pp171–187. Available at: https://doi.org/10.1007/s10672-021-09366-2
This article has eight authors/ researchers: 'et al' used in the text after the first name and all names are listed in the reference.	

How to reference a webpage

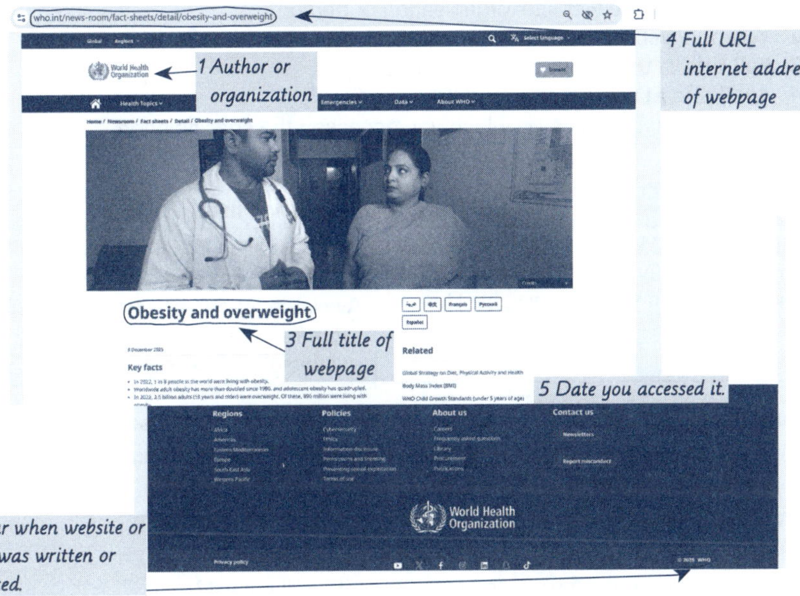

<table>
<tr><td colspan="2">Five points of an online reference</td></tr>
<tr><td colspan="2">

1 **Author**(s) of the website (organisation or person)
2 **Year** the website or page was written or updated
3 **Full title** of the webpage or site (in *italics*)
4 **Available at** https://www … (URL)
5 **(Accessed …)** + date on which you accessed the specific page.
</td></tr>
</table>

In your work	Reference list
The WHO (2025) reports that 160 million children were living with obesity in 2024, and 360 million were overweight. This …	World Health Organization (WHO) (2025). *Obesity and overweight.* Available at: https://www.who.int/news-room/fact-sheets/detail/obesity-and-overweight (Accessed 15 July 2025).

If any of the above details really are missing, then include those you do have. Do some strategic thinking though: what is this source floating around cyberspace with no visible author or organisation?

▸ Who wrote it? A human or AI?
▸ How did they do the research/produce the policy? So …
▸ How reliable is the information? Can I trust it? Will I use it?

 REFERENCING, UNDERSTANDING PLAGIARISM AND ETHICAL AI

Social media

Social media posts are often personal views and experiences. They are also a common form of communicating short reports and updates by many organisations, so can provide useful current evidence for research purposes.

Blog

In your work	Reference list
Urgent action is needed to rethink water use at every level, adopt circular water systems and prepare for future disruptions in water supplies (Brody and González 2025).	Brody S and González D (2025). *A $13 trillion call to action: building water resilience. McKinsey Sustainability Blog,* 29 May. Available at: https://www.mckinsey.com/capabilities/sustainability/our-insights/sustainability-blog/a-13-trillion-call-to-action-building-water-resilience (Accessed 7 June 2025).

LinkedIn

In your work	Reference list
Professional networking through social media does not necessarily result in meaningful connections or relationship-building (Boddy 2025).	Boddy M (2025). *The LinkedIn Paradox: why we're all networking, but few are connecting.* LinkedIn, 6 June. Available at: https://www.linkedin.com/pulse/linkedin-paradox-why-were-all-networking-few-connecting-michael-boddy-wpkte/?trackingId=OSgrqI4 3Q5mLfoNatrW7sQ%3D%3D (Accessed 11 June 2025).

Instagram

In your work	Reference list
World Environment Day (5 June) is designed as a call to action for everyone to protect the world from pollution and act on climate change (UN Climate Change 2025).	UN Climate Change (2025). *Happy World Environment Day!* Instagram. 5 June. Available at: https://www.instagram.com/reel/DKhJWNZsuEQ/?igsh=bDZxcGtjMm1namcz (Accessed 6 June 2025).

 REFERENCING, UNDERSTANDING PLAGIARISM AND ETHICAL AI

Tik Tok

In your work	Reference list
Attempts by environmental organisations to stop mining of the deep sea have had some success (Greenpeace 2023), although …	Greenpeace (2023). #Stopdeepseamining. Tiktok, 24 November. Available at: https://www.tiktok.com/@greenpeacenz/video/7305134739218763010 (Accessed 26 June 2025).

Audiovisual material

Film

In your work	Reference list
A *Minecraft Movie* based on the original video game from 2011 is a successful adaption to live action comedy …(A *Minecraft Movie* 2025).	*A Minecraft Movie* (2025). Directed by Jared Hess [Film]. United States: Warner Bros. Pictures.

YouTube

In your work	Reference list
Charles Duhigg's talk (2024) explaining why people struggle to communicate when their intentions in a conversation do not match …	Duhigg C (2024). *The science behind dramatically better conversations.* Available at: https://www.youtube.com/watch?v=K_RSZC0s8a4 (Accessed 20 June 2025).

Podcast

In your work	Reference list
Joe Patrice referred to current appointees to the US government as 'teenagers' … (Patrice 2025). Whether this is …	Patrice J (2025). *You catch more judges with 'Honey' than with vinegar.* (Podcast). 25 June. Available at: 'Thinking Like a Lawyer': https://legaltalknetwork.com/podcasts/thinking-like-a-lawyer/ (Accessed 1 July 2025)

REFERENCING, UNDERSTANDING PLAGIARISM AND ETHICAL AI

Image

In your work	Reference list
Gross (2024) presents the swarm of life as a huge mass of tadpoles under lily pads in a lake on Vancouver Island.	Gross S (2024). *The swarm of life*. London: Natural History Museum. Available at: https://www.nhm.ac.uk/wpy (Accessed 7 June 2025).

Reports and company / official documentation

Reports

In your work	Reference list
… 62% of consumers have recycled used products in the past 12 months (Mintel 2024) which seems like a low figure considering …	Mintel (2024). *UK ethical retailing and market report*. Available at: https://store.mintel.com/report/uk-ethical-retailing-market-report (Accessed 25 July 2025).

Statistics

In your work	Reference list
Despite a 3.6% reduction in the apparel retail market in Indonesia between 2018 and 2023, the market is predicted to grow by 2028 (Marketline 2024).	Marketline (2024). *Apparel retail in Indonesia*. Available at: https://www.marketresearch.com/MarketLine-v3883/Apparel-Retail-Indonesia-38599447/ (Accessed 5 July 2025).

Legislation

In your work	Reference list
The Equality Act (2010) brought together nine 'protected characteristics' in a single piece of legislation. It has been implemented over time and continues to …	HM Government (2010). *Equality Act 2010, c.15*. Available at: https://www.legislation.gov.uk/ukpga/2010/15/contents (Accessed 24 June 2024).

 REFERENCING, UNDERSTANDING PLAGIARISM AND ETHICAL AI

Personal communications

The primary purpose of referencing personal communications is to record and evidence your research trail in your project, not to enable your reader to track back to the source. It may be more appropriate to include a transcript/edited key points/email as an appendix.

In your work	Reference list
Clarke (2024) offered some additional insights into …	Clarke E (2024). Email to Leila Bancroft. 13 September.
Link to appendix One branch manager commented on the difficulties of … (see Appendix 1)	**Appendix 1: Email correspondence** Elliott Clarke: 13 September 2024 *or* Branch Manager A (if anonymity required)

Becoming a confident researcher

You will by now have identified a broad pattern to the information you need to record a reference for any source you use. A reference is the answer to the **strategic questions** (p9) you ask yourself about any source you encounter:

Who wrote it?
When was it published?
What is the source?
How was it published? What kind of 'host'?
Where did **you** find it? (and where can **I** find it?)

1 Author(s)

Who wrote/created it?

2 Year

When was it published/produced?

3 Title of article

What is the source?

Eaton J, Baingana F, Abdulaziz M, Obindo T, Skuse D, Jenkins R (2023). The negative impact of global health worker migration, and how it can be addressed. *Public Health.* 225, Dec 2023, pp254–257. https://doi.org/10.1016/j.puhe.2023.09.014

5 Volume + Issue   *6 Pages*   *7 doi*   *4 Title of journal*

How did I find it? How can you find it?

You can adapt this to any source you need to reference.

• **Author** (artist / creator / organisation) **•** **Year** of publication **•** **Title of item** you are reading or viewing	**•** **What kind of item?** Article / chapter … medium – image / advertisement / graph / artwork / social media **•** **Title of 'host'**: ebook / journal / website / collection /database / platform **•** **Available / Helpful details** to locate the item: in print / online / physical location

For online materials, include
• **doi** where there is one (generally for articles)
For all other online materials
• **URL + Date you** accessed it.

How do I reference ...?

What do you do if you can't find a model for the source you want to use, or for the changes you have made to a source you located?

You want to be helpful to your reader – give them the details they need to be able to follow your research footprints and find the source you used.

Be confident! Work at it and if you really can't find a model for a particular item, generate it from the outline (and thinking) above.

Present all your references in a consistent order and style. You may find it helpful to use bibliographic software / reference manager (see p. 17) to prompt you to include details in an orderly way.

And the point of it all?

The point is to show your research footprints – to be transparent about what your source is, and helpful to your reader if they want to track it.

Did you spot the missing 'strategic question'? **WHY?** Why is the writer writing? What is their purpose? Their argument? This may prompt you to ask more questions: how good is their research? What evidence do they draw on? How will you draw on their work? At this point you are becoming a critical thinker, a competent and successful student and researcher, able to make ethical use of AI, with your own perspective and your own voice.

Enjoy!

 REFERENCING, UNDERSTANDING PLAGIARISM AND ETHICAL AI

Appendix: Other styles of referencing

This Appendix is designed to offer you models for three referencing styles widely used in universities (in addition to Harvard, used throughout this book):

In-text numerical styles:
- Numeric (Vancouver): Appendix A
- MHRA: Appendix B

In-text author style:
- APA: Appendix C

Each extract is specially written to offer you a taste of how the style works, as well as incorporating some of the most used reference formats for each style – take a close look!

All examples show
- how to make the link from your text (**citation**) to the source (**reference**)
- where **footnotes** are used, how to detail a source here
- how to set out references in the **reference list** (or **'bibliography'** or **'Works Cited'**).

Look closely at the annotations: they have been carefully constructed to offer useful models, for both the writing and in citing references.

For more on any specific style, a simple search will take you to various university library websites around the world. Check two – but be prepared for variations. Even within guidance on the same style, individual course/module handbooks, institutions, journals and online advice will vary. So:

- get the general idea of how to use a particular style (from this book)
- use any guidance you are given in your course materials or library
- consider using bibliographic software / a reference manager (see p. 17) to keep track of your references and ensure you present them consistently and accurately.

Appendix A: Numeric (Vancouver) style

Numeric (Vancouver): in-text numeric style + references in number order

Numeric referencing styles are most commonly used in science, medicine and related subjects and minimise distractions on the page. References have logical but minimal punctuation and no unnecessary words to distract from the communication.

Numeric styles, including Vancouver, work like this:

- **In your work** use a number in superscript[3] or brackets, round (3) or square [3], at the point where you draw on a source.
- **In your references** give the full details of each source in numerical order, with the first source you use listed as 1, the second as 2 and so on.
- **Each source keeps its number** however many times you use it. It is only listed once in your references. In the extract below, references 3 and 15 are cited more than once.

Below is the same extract (adapted) from the article by Eaton et al. (Chapter 5) using the numeric (Vancouver) reference style of the original article.

Academic literature spanning decades has documented the damage that the medical brain-drain does to health services in poorer countries[3]. WHO reports have repeatedly drawn attention to the critical shortages of health workers across Africa, the Middle East and Asia[4,5]. Most LMICs have much poorer health indices than OECD countries[14], and the WHO has estimated that countries with less than 23 health workers per 10,000 population are unable to deliver essential health services[3,15].

…International recruitment of medical staff is, in many instances, creating a subsidy from poor to richer countries[6,15] …

Reference to source 3 in the reference list

Reference to two sources supporting this point

Reference to another study with points of relevance to the argument

Further reference to source 3 and another source supporting this point

New paragraph, new point in argument and supporting evidence

All six authors listed.

Eaton J, Baingana F, Abdulaziz M, Obindo T, Skuse D, Jenkins R (2023). The negative impact of global health worker migration, and how it can be addressed. *Public Health*. 225, Dec 2023, pp254–257. Available at: https://doi.org/10.1016/j.puhe.2023.09.014.

REFERENCING, UNDERSTANDING PLAGIARISM AND ETHICAL AI

Selected references for this extract

<table>
<tr><td>3</td><td>Beine M, Docquier F, Rapoport H. Brain drain and human capital formation in developing countries: winners and losers. Econ J. 2008:118 (528): 631–652. Available at: https://doi.org/10.1111/j.1468-0297.2008.02135.x</td></tr>
<tr><td>4,5</td><td>(not detailed here)</td></tr>
<tr><td>14</td><td>WHO. Global strategy on human resources for health: Workforce 2030. Geneva: World Health Organization. 2016. Accessed 27 June 2025.</td></tr>
</table>

3 Journal article (print and online)
- *Three authors*
- *Title of article (standard text)*
- *Title of journal (often shortened as here)*
- *Year of publication*
- *Volume of journal in bold*
- *Page numbers just as numbers*
- *Article identifier: doi or e number*

4,5 Evidence to support the point

14 Organisation as author
- *Author*
- *Title of source*
- *Place of publication + publisher*
- *Year of publication*
- *Date accessed*

Appendix B: MHRA style (Modern Humanities Research Association)

MHRA: in-text numeric style + footnotes in number order + Bibliography

This referencing style is used in some arts and humanities subjects. It allows readers to see immediately the source of information or to get a glimpse of a discussion point on the same page as the text.

The citation in the text makes the link to the footnote with a **number**, usually in **superscript**[1].

Sources are first shown in **footnotes** at the bottom of the page, in the order in which they occur throughout the essay or article, or, less often, as **endnotes** at the end. All sources, and other sources read but not cited, are collected together in a full **bibliography** at the end.

This example has been written to show how this referencing style works. It is not a good piece of writing, and has far too many references. Some are even fictional!

In your work

The popularity of the cinema peaked in the 1940s and 1950s.[1] It remained above 1,000 million between 1940 and 1955.[2] Precise figures about audiences are hard to come by,[3] but it is clear that the majority of cinema-goers were women.[4] Hollywood carried out research that established that women wanted 'good character development' and 'human interest'.[5] The films produced by Hollywood at this time were 'strongly feminised'[6] and appealed to their largely female audiences for their 'glamour'[7] ... Some women watched particular films – such as *Calamity Jane* – countless times ...[8]

In your footnotes (or endnotes)

1 Pat Fisher and Piers Madison, *The Cinema Compendium*, (London: British Film Association, 1999), pp219–20.
2 Ibid., p209.
3 For a useful collection of facts and figures of cinema-going Britain, see Melvyn Wallerstein, 'Going to the pictures: the changing social experience', *The Cinema Journal*, 35 (2018), 103–115.
4 *The Cinema Compendium*, p225.
5 Ibid., p220.
6 *Frank Dubon, Hollywood Revisited,* (New York: Studio Panorama, 2014), p158.
7 Ibid., p167.
8 These films have provoked considerable debate among
....

Footnotes explained

A book (first mention), full details:
- *First names before surnames for up to three authors;*
- *'and others' for four or more authors*
- *Title in italics*
- *Other details in brackets (place of publication, publisher, year)*
- *Page number(s) last: p for one page, pp for more than one page*
- *Commas used throughout and full stop at the end.*

'Ibid' is short for the Latin 'ibidem' meaning 'in the same place'. It refers to the source immediately before (Pat Fisher and Piers Madison).

A short discussion of the difficulties of finding reliable information, and refers the reader to a book listed in the bibliography (Wallerstein), but not cited in the text.

A quick referral back to a source already cited in full.

This refers to The Cinema Compendium again. See (1) for full details.

Another source, full details

This refers to the source immediately above – Dubon.

This is the beginning of a lengthy note summarising the discussion among commentators.

 REFERENCING, UNDERSTANDING PLAGIARISM AND ETHICAL AI

In your bibliography at the end, you collect all the sources from your footnotes, and list them in alphabetical order.

Bibliography	Your bibliography explained
Dubon, Frank, *Hollywood Revisited*, (New York: Studio Panorama, 2014)	*Note the 'hanging indent': the first line of each work cited goes to the margin, and the rest is indented.* *A book, one author, with full details:* *- Surname first (first name in full or initials)* *- Title in italics* *- Other details in brackets (place of publication, publisher, year)* *- No page numbers* *- Commas used throughout, no full stop at the end.*
Fisher, Pat and Piers Madison, *The Cinema Compendium*, (London: British Film Association, 1999)	*A book, two authors* *Full details as above (surname first for first author), then first name first for second and third + authors.*
Wallerstein, Melvyn, 'Going to the pictures: the changing social experience', *The Cinema Journal*, 35 (2010), 103–115	*Journal article* *This article is not directly referenced in the essay, but was used as background reading. Include it in the bibliography, with full details:* *- Author, surname first* *- Title of article in single quotation marks* *- Title of journal in italics* *- Details in brackets (volume/issue)* *- Year of publication* *- Page numbers* *- Give the doi if it has one* *- Or give the URL like this:* *<www.jstor.org/stable/644897> [Accessed 27 March 2026]*

Appendix C: APA style (American Psychological Association)

APA: in-text author/year + References in alphabetical order

This style is used in subjects related to psychology and in some other social science subject areas. It is similar to Harvard.

The extract and comments below illustrate where APA is **different** to Harvard.

In your work

> … oral language skills underpin successful reading comprehension (Garcia, Martin, Gauson & Misra, 2018; Lopez & Hulme, 2020). The National Institute for Reading (NIR) (2022) set out the evidence for early engagement with picture books. Lopez and Hulme argue that talking about picture books enables children to make the transition to reading …. Garcia et al. underline the importance of … Children who have experience of wordless picture books have learnt to read images (Keenan et al., 2019), a skill they carry into …

Your in-text references explained

Three to five authors
- List all in your text the first time you refer to them with the last linked by '&'
- Later citations, shorten to first author followed by 'et al.'

One or two authors
- Give the surname (for one), or both surnames (linked with & for two) throughout your work

Organisation as author
- Give name in full the first time you mention it, and by initials for subsequent citations

- Use 'and' (not '&') to link two authors when the names fall naturally in the sentence.
- No need to repeat the year of publication when you refer to the same author in the same paragraph

Six or more authors
- Shorten to first author's surname + 'et al.' throughout

References

Garcia, P., Martin, S.G., Gauson, M.D. & Misra, K.B. (2018). Talk first: laying the foundations for reading. *Reading research, 35(7),* pp346–78. Available at: https://doi.org/10.1288/0945167331057081

Keenan, F., Muter, S.R., Linden, K., Schmitt, R., Johnson, J. & Elster, M.A. (2019). Assessing reading comprehension in young children. In A. Goodman (Ed.), *Learning the language* (pp77–95). Boston: Parton.

National Institute for Reading (NIR) (2022). *Teaching reading: an evidence based assessment of strategies for teaching reading.* Retrieved from www.nir.org.uk/data/teachread/file/pdf

Your reference list explained

Journal article
- Three to five authors, last linked with '&'
- Year of publication (in brackets)
- Title of article
- Title of journal + volume and issue in italics
- DOI

Chapter in book
- Six authors, the maximum given in full before using et al.
- Year
- Chapter title
- In
- Author or editor of book with initial(s) first. Note (Ed.) or (Eds.)
- Title of book in italics
- Pages
- [Place of publication:] publisher

Organisation as author/online report
- Name of organisation in full and by initials
- Title of publication in italics
- Retrieved from [URL] No date given

REFERENCING, UNDERSTANDING PLAGIARISM AND ETHICAL AI

References

Committee on Publication Ethics [COPE] (2023). *COPE position - Authorship and AI Tools - English*. Available at: https://doi.org/10.24318/cCVRZBms

Henderson E (2025). Using AI to track down leftovers. *UNESCO Courier*, 2/4/25. Available at: https://courier.unesco.org/en/articles/using-ai-track-down-leftovers

Oxford University Press (2007). *The Shorter Oxford English Dictionary*. 6th edn.

The Open University (2008). *Thinking critically*. Available at: https://studenthublive.open.ac.uk/sites/studenthublive.open.ac.uk/files/files/thinking-critically.pdf (Accessed 7 October 2025)

University of Manchester (2023). *Academic Phrasebank: referring to sources*. Available at: https://www.phrasebank.manchester.ac.uk/ (Accessed 21 July 2025).

European Network for Academic Integrity [ENAI] (2023). *Database of educational materials.* Available at: https://academicintegrity.eu/materials/

King's College London (2025). *Generative AI: student guidance*. Available at: https://www.kcl.ac.uk/about/strategy/learning-and-teaching/ai-guidance/student-guidance

QAA (2023). *The improvement of student learning by linking inclusion/accessibility and academic integrity.* Project resources available at: https://www.qaa.ac.uk//en/membership/collaborative-enhancement-projects/academic-integrity/the-improvement-of-student-learning-by-linking-inclusion-accessibility-and-academic-integrity

UCL Library Services (2025). *Why use reference management software?* Available at: https://library-guides.ucl.ac.uk/reference-management-software/why

UNESCO (2023). *Guidance for generative AI in education and research*. Available at: https://unesdoc.unesco.org/ark:/48223/pf0000386693

Related books in the Pocket Study Skills series

Coonan E (2020). *Where's Your Evidence?* Bloomsbury.

Godfrey J (2023). *Reading and Making Notes.* 3rd edn. Bloomsbury.

Godwin J (2025). *Planning Your Essay.* 4th edn. Bloomsbury.

Van Der Ham V and Heyliger J (2026). *Doing Your Literature Review*. Bloomsbury.

Williams K (2022). *Getting Critical.* 3rd edn. Bloomsbury.

Williams K and Reid M (2023). *Planning Your Dissertation.* 3rd edn. Bloomsbury.

Index